Tell Your Cat You're Pregnant
An essential guide for cat owners who are expecting a baby

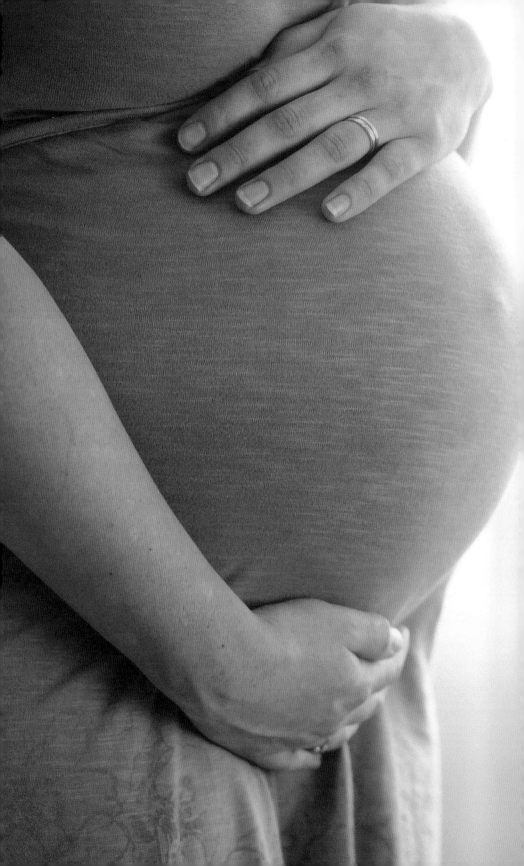

Tell Your Cat You're Pregnant

An essential guide for cat owners who are expecting a baby

Dr Lewis Kirkham

BVSc MRCVS MANZCVS(Animal Behaviour)

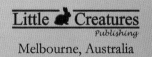

Little Creatures Publishing

Melbourne, Australia

Published by Little Creatures Publishing Pty Ltd (csc2015pb)
PO Box 777, Port Melbourne, Victoria, Australia 3207

Cover by Gigi and Lulu / Typesetting by Nada Backovic Designs
Photos: shutterstock.com, istockphoto.com

National Library of Australia Cataloguing-in-Publication entry:
Tell Your Cat You're Pregnant: an essential guide for cat owners who are expecting a baby (includes downloadable MP3 sounds) (CD not included)
/Lewis Kirkham.
1st ed.
ISBN 9780987053084 (paperback)
Cats--Behavior.
Cats--Effect of human beings on.
Pregnancy--Popular works.
636.80887

Disclaimer
This publication intends to provide accurate and authoritative information about the subject matter within. While all care has been taken to ensure that it is accurate, the author and/or the publisher: expressly disclaim responsibility for any errors, omissions or adverse effects arising from the use or application of the information contained herein, make no representation or warranty, express or implied, as to the accuracy, effectiveness, completeness, reasonableness, fitness, merchantability or reliability of the information contained in this publication, do not accept any liability for injury or loss (including consequential loss), expense of any nature arising directly or indirectly from the application of, use of or reliance on this publication or any information derived from or omitted from this publication, and shall not be liable for any loss of profit or any other commercial damages, including but not limited to special, incidental, consequential or other damages.

This publication contains information and advice that is current at the time of printing. Cats, babies and children are unpredictable: there can be no guarantees for cat behaviour any more than there can for human behaviour. Please do not follow any advice in this book unless it makes perfect sense to you, and *never leave your cat and baby or child together unsupervised*.

This publication and the techniques and suggestions are to be used at the reader's discretion and should not be a substitute for the advice of your doctor, physician, health-care provider or veterinarian.

If you do not wish to be bound by the above, you may return this book to the place of purchase or to the publisher for a full refund.

All breeds of cats and names of people and cats within this book have been changed to protect privacy.

To my dearly loved,
caring and supportive mother.
I see you every day in the mirror.

Acknowledgements

Thank you to my wife, Deb, not only for her assistance with this book but also for being the light and love of my life and keeping me on an even keel.

Thank you to my daughters, Stella and April, for your love and the fun we have together but also for your ideas about the book and editorial assistance.

Special thanks go to my father, Colin, for his continued love, voice of reason and editorial support.

Professionally, I would like to thank my first-grade teacher who said I would either be Prime Minister of Australia or end up in jail.

I wish to express my appreciation to my colleagues Dr Nick Branson, Dr Debbie Calnon, Dr Sally Nixon and Dr Katrina Ward for their contributions. A special thankyou goes to Dr David Lindsay for reviewing the chapter on Toxoplasmosis.

Thank you also to Nicola Redhouse and Nan McNab for their editorial assistance.

"As an obstetrician, parent and cat owner I highly recommend *Tell Your Cat You're Pregnant* to all cat owners who are expecting a baby. It provides valuable information on the important topic of toxoplasmosis and pregnancy, as well as comprehensively detailing how best to prepare a cat for a new baby. Dr Kirkham also thoroughly covers the common myths and issues that are often raised regarding cats and pregnancy, which makes for interesting and enjoyable reading."

Dr Sally Reid MB BS FRANZCOG
Consultant Obstetrician & Gynaecologist

"As feline veterinarians, we are often asked questions by expectant parents nervous about the introduction of their new baby to their feline family. Dr Kirkham's book has the *purrfect* answers to these and many other medical and household questions that will help prepare your cat for the arrival of a baby. Cat parents who are expecting will find this book an invaluable support and reference. We highly recommend it."

Dr Amy Lingard BVSc(Hons) FACVSc
Registered Feline Medicine Specialist
Dr Richard Gowan BVSc(Hons) MACVSc
The Cat Clinic, Melbourne Australia

"As an obstetrician and cat owner, I applaud Dr Kirkham's comprehensive, practical and well organised approach to introducing a new baby to a resident cat. Dr Kirkham covers many of the health issues that may occur regarding cats and babies including a thorough section on pregnancy and toxoplasmosis."

Dr Gene-Lyn Ngian MBBS B Med Sci
Obstetrics & Gynaecology Registrar

Contents

Introduction   13

1   The benefits of being owned by a cat   19

2   Common myths and problems   25

3   Toxoplasmosis   35

4   Aggression   53

5   Toileting issues   69

5   Knowing your cat   85

7   Sounds like a baby!   103

8   Supervising, separating and training   121

9   Staying healthy   143

10 Preparing your cat   159

11 Are you ready?   179

12 Your baby is born!   185

    Further help   207

    Tell us about your experience   209

    About the author   211

Introduction

Do you have a much-loved cat? Your 'fur kid'? Are you expecting or trying for a baby and want to prepare your cat for the new family member with minimal stress? If so, this book is for you. It includes 13 soundtracks of baby and toy noises specifically designed to prepare your cat for your baby's arrival.* Each track contains sounds that will be new to your home when your baby arrives. With the help of these, and the information in this book, you and your cat will handle the change to a larger family happily and successfully. Remember, cats who are properly prepared usually adjust to the new family member smoothly.

It is important to read the entire book before playing any of the tracks to your cat. By all means play the sounds to yourself, but _not_ to your cat until you are ready to work through the program.

Early preparation

Whether you are trying for a baby or about to have a baby, there are many things you can do early on to prepare yourself and your cat for this important change in the family. Preparing early gives your cat more time to adjust to most of the changes in the household, short of your baby actually arriving. If your cat is not adjusting well to these early prenatal household changes, then at least you will know that it is not the baby who is causing the problem.

* The baby and toy sounds can be downloaded free as MP3 tracks from http://goo.gl/tYpnZb

Who needs this book?

If you are an expectant parent as well as a cat owner, this book is for you.* It contains advice on health issues regarding your pregnancy, baby and cat. You will also find helpful advice for managing your cat's interactions with your baby from before the birth until roughly baby's first birthday (when babies become more mobile). While many people find their cat is friendly and gentle around older children or adults, cats can react quite differently to the noises and movements of a small baby.

If you are likely to have a baby as a visitor, whether you are a friend, grandparent, aunt, uncle or other relative of an expectant family, this book can also help. So remember to pass it on to any cat owner who is likely to be involved with your new baby. Or, better still, buy them their own copy!

This book will also help to identify when you may need further professional advice. Any reference to an 'appropriate veterinarian' means veterinarians with a professional interest in animal behaviour.

> Most cats smoothly adjust to the arrival of a new baby if prepared in advance

Babies and your cat

If your cat has never spent much time around babies, it is a good idea to begin exposing them to the sights, sounds and smells of a newborn. While this is a great idea in theory, it is not easy to achieve in practice. This is where *Tell Your Cat You're Pregnant* will greatly assist you.

Try to recall if your cat has had previous exposure to young babies or, next time you invite friends or family members with babies to your

*If you also own a dog then you need to read *Tell Your Dog You're Pregnant: An essential guide for dog owners who are expecting a baby.*

home, pay special attention to your cat. How did they react? If your cat reacted unfavourably, you have some work to do, and you may even require the assistance of an appropriate veterinarian. But this book is a great first step. Even if your cat reacts favourably to babies, it is still best to take all relevant precautions, as the consequences of being wrong can, occasionally, be devastating. Do not alarm yourself though; remember, most cats quickly and easily adjust to the arrival of a new baby if they are prepared in advance.

How an individual cat responds to a new baby will depend upon its personality and temperament, past experience and current environment. Some cats will adapt quickly to new babies and immediately be inquisitive, playful or affectionate. Others will ignore them. While investigation and affection are desirable, these behaviours must be well supervised, as they can still lead to injury for the baby; similarly, sudden movements or noises from the baby could scare your cat. Some cats can become anxious or fearful due to the presence of a baby, causing them to have toileting issues or to begin hiding for long periods. Occasionally, a particularly fearful cat may become aggressive. Fear can lead to persistent avoidance or aggression if it's not treated promptly and correctly.

It is important to prepare your cat early for what could well be the biggest change in their life. But with the right advice and preparation, cats, pregnancy and babies can all go together without a hitch.

The evil household appliance

Barb rang me sounding quite desperate. 'You've got to help me. Cleo, the cat, is annoyed by our new baby and she's taking it out on us! She's urinating all over the house.'

I scheduled an urgent house call for the next day.

As I rang the doorbell, I could hear a baby crying and Barb answered carrying her gorgeous new baby, Chelsea. Barb explained that it was Chelsea's nap time and gestured for me to take a seat in the living room. As soon as I sat down, Cleo, a very friendly British Blue, jumped onto my lap and made herself comfortable while I petted her. She did not seem upset by the crying coming from the other room and was focused on my attention. When the crying ceased, Barb emerged and we started to chat.

When Chelsea first came home, the introductions had gone smoothly and everything seemed to be going well. A few weeks later, Cleo suddenly started urinating in odd areas around the house. She would still use the litter box for faeces, but never for urine. And, interestingly, she would only use the box for faeces at night. I asked Barb to show me the areas around the house that Cleo was now using. The three of us – Barb, Cleo and I – began a tour of the house. Cleo was now using three different areas in the house to toilet. One was under the desk in the study. The second was behind the door of a spare bedroom, and the third was in the shower in the upstairs bathroom, which was never used. They all seemed to be secluded locations, as if Cleo was trying to get away from the baby. I could see how Barb could link Cleo's behaviour with Chelsea's arrival.

Continuing our tour of the house, I asked Barb to show me where the litter box was located. Cleo and I followed her into the laundry. We chatted further, about exciting topics such as litter-box cleaning and hygiene, while Barb absent-mindedly loaded the washing machine with baby clothes and turned it on. This was all normal for a multi-tasking mother, but Cleo's response to the sound of the washing machine was remarkable. She bolted out of the laundry and disappeared under the bed in the spare room – she clearly did not enjoy the noise. Barb explained that she had seen her do this a few times. One time, she had accidently put a plastic toy in the machine, which had made a horrible noise. This really scared Cleo, and she had stayed under the bed in the spare room for an entire day.

In that moment, the issue became reasonably clear to me. Cleo was not annoyed with the presence of Chelsea and taking revenge on her owners by urinating everywhere. She was now scared of the washing machine and was looking for a quieter place to urinate. The fact that she would only use the litter box for faeces at night, when the washing machine was silent, also made sense.

We discussed moving the existing litter box into the upstairs spare bathroom, and adding another litter box in the spare bedroom. In the future, if one of the boxes was not used at all by Cleo, Barb could possibly remove it; but it would be good to have a spare box in case one of the rooms was occupied or not accessible at some time.

I dropped in to see Barb, Chelsea and Cleo three months later. Barb was flustered because Chelsea had colic and was not sleeping very well. Cleo clearly wasn't bothered at all by the obvious stress in the house and proceeded to rub her head and body on my leg with an audible purr. I asked Barb how the urinating was going and she said, in a blasé manner, 'Ah, all fine. She uses the litter box in the spare bathroom just perfectly now.' This news was music to my ears – I was so pleased I could help Barb focus on her precious baby rather than on cleaning up after Cleo.

1
The benefits of being owned by a cat

The relationship between children and their cat is special and comforting, and it brings with it many benefits for child development, family harmony and even health.

Social benefits

Having a relationship with a cat can help develop skills such as:

- ❖ empathy
- ❖ ability to care and nurture
- ❖ responsibility
- ❖ non-verbal communication.

Studies have shown that children with cats:

- ❖ have higher self-esteem
- ❖ have improved social skills
- ❖ are more popular and empathetic with their peers
- ❖ have less time off school due to illness.

Cats are a source of companionship and enjoyment for many people. Pets teach children important lessons about life, and provide unconditional love and a safe outlet for confidences otherwise left unspoken. Pets can provide comfort and support for children living in stressful situations or enduring periods of hardship.

Owning a cat is beneficial for the whole family, and families with a pet:

❖ interact more and have reduced stress levels
❖ are more likely to engage in fun activities, friendly conversations and conversations about important topics

> Owning a cat is beneficial
> for the whole family

Health benefits

Animal companionship yields many health benefits. For example, your chances of surviving for at least one year after a stay in a hospital with heart problems are much greater if you own a pet. Members of pet-owning families are more likely to have normal levels of immune function than those family members who don't own pets. Pet ownership has been shown to reduce elevated blood pressure caused by stress more effectively than medication. Pet owners have lower blood pressure and resting heart rates, and show a faster return to normal levels of both of these after stress.

Babies in early contact with cats or dogs are 30 per cent less likely to experience coughs, ear infections and symptoms such as runny nose, sneezing and congestion.

Compared to their petless counterparts, pet owners:

❖ have lower blood pressure and cholesterol levels
❖ have a decreased risk of cardiovascular disease and a decreased risk of death due to heart attacks and stroke
❖ have fewer minor illnesses and complaints and visit the doctor less often
❖ have improved moods and decreased psychological distress, depression and loneliness

2
Common myths and problems

Common myths exposed

Expectant parents are bombarded with advice, and the subject of cats is no exception. Some of this advice can be wrong, extreme, or based on ignorance or folklore. In the past pregnant women were advised to avoid cats completely and, unfortunately, people still give away or abandon cats merely because they are expecting a baby.

> Expectant parents are often bombarded with advice about cats and pregnancy

'Your cat will intentionally smother or 'suck the breath out' of your baby ...'

There is much hearsay about cats smothering babies in their cots or cribs or placing their mouth over the baby's mouth to 'suck their breath out' and extract the baby's 'magic'; or, slightly less bizarrely, to suck out the baby's milk. While many cats like to drink (cow's) milk, there is no evidence to suggest that cats actively try to get at milk within a baby's mouth. Suggestions that a cat will 'suck the breath out' of a baby while it is sleeping seem to stem from centuries-old folklore, when cats were considered evil and part of witchery or black magic.

It is possible that a cat might accidentally smother a baby, because cats do like to seek out warm and comfortable areas to rest, and could easily nestle up against a sleeping infant and accidentally obstruct the airway. There has only ever been one documented proven case worldwide in the last few decades where an infant's cause of death was attributed to being smothered by a cat. Cat fur was found in the infant's throat on autopsy. While it may seem alarming that a cat could accidentally smother a baby, the risk is exceptionally low. And there is nothing to suggest cats do this on purpose. In the past, the smothering of babies by cats has been documented in reports; however, most of these are prior to 1969 when Sudden Infant Death Syndrome (SIDS) was first identified and named. Often a cat was found nearby, probably leading to the assumption that the cat caused the death. Subsequent autopsies have often highlighted SIDS or another cause for the baby's death.

Nevertheless, it is worth remembering that there is a small possibility that a cat could smother an infant who is not strong enough to move its head away from a cat seeking warmth and comfort. For this reason, cats should never be allowed unsupervised in the same room as a sleeping or unattended baby, irrespective of whether the baby is in a stroller, pram, portable cot or crib, baby swing, or anything else. Interactions between cats and babies should always be supervised and if this is not possible then they should be separated.

'You need to get rid of your cat when you are pregnant because cats have toxoplasma ...'

One of the most common pieces of inaccurate advice is about the risk of catching toxoplasmosis from your cat. In fact, toxoplasmosis can easily be avoided *without* getting rid of your cat (see Chapter 3: Toxoplasmosis).

> Toxoplasmosis can easily be avoided without getting rid of your cat

'The cat is jealous and might be aggressive …'

Many cat owners claim the most common emotion displayed by their cat when a baby arrives is jealousy — the cat is 'put out' by the newcomer. In fact, the cat is probably feeling anxious, not jealous. Much of this anxiety is associated with sudden changes to its routine and environment. For this reason, it is important to start preparing your cat as early as possible for your baby's arrival. The longer lead time you have to introduce changes to the household, the less disruption there will be for your cat when your baby comes home.

'I am worried my cat will claw my baby's eyes out …'

It might sound like a bizarre comment, but this is a common concern. Cat aggression (scratching or biting) towards newborns is rare but frightening. The majority of cats are scared of babies, and their first response is usually to hide from the baby. Cats can also be aggressive towards children if cornered or in pain. If your cat currently displays aggression in any circumstances you should immediately seek the assistance of an appropriate veterinarian.

Common problems

If your cat has any behavioural issues, work on resolving them before the baby's birth. Afterwards, you'll be distracted and focused on your baby's needs and the cat's behaviour issues will be more difficult to tackle. Worse, the arrival of the new little one may exacerbate the problem. Common problems include: toileting outside the litter box, urine spraying or marking, and excessive hiding, scratching or biting. *Tell Your Cat You're Pregnant* will help you to reduce or eliminate those problems before your baby arrives. A consultation with an appropriate veterinarian may also be needed.

'My cat is peeing around the house ...'

Toileting issues are one of the most common problems that surface when a cat owner becomes pregnant or brings home a new baby. They can be divided into:

- ❖ toileting outside the litter box (that is, urine and sometimes faeces deposited anywhere around the house); or
- ❖ urine spraying or marking.

Often owners believe that their cat is doing this to be spiteful or because they are jealous of the new baby. In fact, a cat will toilet outside the litter box because of their own preferences or dislikes and not because of personal grievances. Urine spraying is a normal form of feline communication, not an act of vengeance, and is usually associated with stress or anxiety (for example, the arrival of a new baby or changes in routine associated with a new baby) (see Chapter 5: Toileting issues).

> **Start preparing your cat as soon as possible for your baby's arrival**

'My cat is meowing and scratching at the bedroom door ...'

Any sudden changes to a cat's environment and/or routine can cause them anxiety. This can lead to problems such as excessive meowing, toileting issues or pacing. If your cat was allowed to sleep in the bedroom or nursery prior to the arrival of the baby but suddenly this is no longer allowed, they may meow and scratch at the door to try to reach their favourite spot. *Tell Your Cat You're Pregnant* will enable you to make changes early so that your cat has plenty of time to adjust before the baby arrives.

'My cat is scared of the baby. She's hiding under the bed and won't come out ...'

Many cats are worried by or even scared of babies. They may not like the sounds, smells and movements babies make, or they may simply be unaccustomed to them. *Tell Your Cat You're Pregnant* explains in detail how to prepare your cat for a baby (without a baby actually being present) so your cat is less likely to be fearful when your baby does arrive. It discusses how to create good emotional associations with the baby, rather than fear. It also highlights the early warning signs that may indicate your cat will be excessively fearful of your baby, allowing you to seek assistance from an appropriate veterinarian.

3
Toxoplasmosis

Toxoplasmosis in humans

Disclaimer: This advice is general and is no substitute for advice from your doctor, physician or health-care provider.

If you're like most expectant parents, you'll be concerned about the health of your unborn child. Sometimes it seems there are hazards everywhere – even from beloved pets. Toxoplasmosis can strike fear into the heart of a pregnant cat owner. It's one of the best known of the diseases humans can catch from animals, but few people really understand what it is, how dangerous it can be, and how to avoid it. *You are at no greater risk of contracting toxoplasmosis if you own a cat.* The good news is, it's easy to protect yourself from this disease, and that means you can keep your beloved cat!

> **You are at no greater risk of contracting toxoplasmosis if you own a cat**

Firstly, the risk of catching toxoplasmosis from a household cat is extremely small and that risk can be further minimised with good basic hygiene. Most people with toxoplasmosis are not infected by their cat but by eating undercooked meat, or poor hygiene or gardening.

Toxoplasmosis is a complex topic – there is a lot of scientific information available and much of it is beyond the scope of this book. However, the following information is usually regarded as crucial to avoiding toxoplasma infection. More extensive information about toxoplasmosis may be viewed at **www.babyandpet.com.au.** Your password to access this is 'detailed chapter'.

What is toxoplasmosis?

Toxoplasmosis is caused by a microscopic parasite called *Toxoplasma gondii*, which is found worldwide. Infection can occur in almost all warm-blooded animals, not just cats and humans.

In people, infection is rarely noticed, as only 20 per cent of people will show symptoms, which are similar to influenza or a bad cold.

Once a person is infected they are infected for life. There is no 'cure' for the infection. Toxoplasma cannot be transmitted from person to person. The exception is when a woman becomes infected with toxoplasma for the first time during pregnancy and she passes the infection on to her unborn child in utero.

Cats are particularly important in the life cycle of toxoplasma because they are the only animal in which the parasite produces tiny 'eggs' (or oocysts) in their faeces. Any animal or person who accidentally ingests these eggs in the cat's faeces, or anything contaminated with these faeces, may contract toxoplasmosis.

It is vital to understand that when cats are *first* infected with toxoplasma they will produce eggs in their faeces for about one to three weeks, and rarely shed eggs again, even if the cat is reinfected. Eggs can be found in the faeces of feral, stray and domestic cats.

In people and all animals except cats, toxoplasma infection causes small cysts to form in the muscles (meat) and brain. Toxoplasma can also be transmitted to people (and cats) when eating or preparing undercooked meat containing these cysts.

> Most people with toxoplasmosis
> are not infected by their cat

How you catch it

Humans catch toxoplasma in three main ways:

1. Eating cysts in raw or undercooked meat and shellfish, unpasteurised milk or unpasteurised milk products;
2. Ingesting eggs from cat faeces or something contaminated with cat faeces, for example soil, sand, cat litter, water, unwashed fruits, salads or vegetables; or
3. A newly infected pregnant woman passing the infection to her unborn baby via the placenta.

The most common method of contracting the disease in the developed world is eating or preparing undercooked infected meat, particularly lamb, pork and venison. Other common sources are drinking contaminated water and exposure to garden soil or sandboxes or sandpits where cats may have defecated.

> **The most common method of contracting toxoplasma is eating or preparing undercooked infected meat**

Overseas travel may expose you to different strains of toxoplasma, so discuss this with your doctor before travelling.

Toxoplasmosis can be of particular concern if you are immune-compromised. If you fall into this category, it is best to talk to your treating doctor.

How you don't catch it

You cannot catch toxoplasmosis by petting, handling or playing with your cat or being scratched or bitten by your cat, because the organism is not spread by the fur or saliva. Transmission directly from cat faeces to humans is quite rare (nobody intentionally eats cat faeces!).

It's very unlikely that an older, healthy cat will be shedding eggs, and it's also unlikely that an indoor cat, fed commercial cat food, will have toxoplasmosis.

Toxoplasma does not live on cat fur. Even when cats are shedding eggs in their faeces, eggs cannot be found on their coat.

> **You cannot catch toxoplasmosis by petting your cat**

Why toxoplasmosis is dangerous for pregnant women

Toxoplasmosis can have serious implications in pregnant woman for their foetus. A woman who becomes infected with toxoplasma for the first time during pregnancy can pass the infection to her unborn baby. This is called congenital toxoplasmosis and the symptoms in the baby vary in severity but may include premature birth, eye problems and seizures. Therefore, it is very important to talk with your doctor before and during your pregnancy about the risk factors associated with toxoplasmosis, including being a cat owner.

Tests for toxoplasmosis

If you are planning a pregnancy, your doctor might recommend, or you might consider, being tested for toxoplasma antibodies. These tests are not always accurate and can be difficult to interpret.

If you have antibodies, it means you have already had the infection, and the risk to your baby of toxoplasmosis is really low.

If you do not have toxoplasmosis antibodies, then your baby is most at risk if you catch toxoplasma while you are pregnant. You are in the group of women who need to take the most precautions and you should seek further assistance from your doctor.

Do not assume that if you have owned cats all your life you will have already contracted toxoplasma, because humans rarely catch it directly from household cats.

Treatments

If you are infected while you are pregnant there is medication to reduce the likelihood that your baby will be infected. Early treatment is more successful. Talk to your doctor if you suspect you may have become infected. No vaccines currently exist to prevent toxoplasmosis.

How do I avoid catching toxoplasmosis from my cat?

Unless your doctor tells you that you are not at risk, assume that you are, and do all you can to avoid infection throughout your pregnancy. Below are some ways to further minimise the low risk of catching toxoplasma from your cat.

- ❖ Cats should ideally be confined inside. Outdoor cats are more likely to have toxoplasmosis than cats who remain strictly indoors, particularly those cats that like to scavenge and hunt outside. Good rodent and pest control around the house reduces the exposure of cats to toxoplasma.
- ❖ Feed your cat dry or canned commercial (cooked) food only.
- ❖ The entire litter box contents (litter, faeces and urine) should be disposed of in a sealed plastic bag daily while wearing gloves. Ideally your partner should do it and place it in a rubbish bin or trash can for disposal. Do not just scoop the litter.
- ❖ Elevate the litter box so your dog (and older more mobile children) cannot reach it.
- ❖ Deter stray or foreign cats, which may be shedding toxoplasma, from visiting your garden.
- ❖ Do not adopt stray cats or a new kitten when you are pregnant as they are more likely to be shedding eggs than a resident adult cat.
- ❖ Excellent hand hygiene is critical. Toxoplasmosis is only a risk if you accidentally 'eat' cat faeces when a cat is shedding eggs. This usually means that you have cat faeces on your hands when you prepare a meal or touch your mouth.

> **Excellent hand hygiene is critical**

How do I avoid toxoplasma infection altogether?

- ❖ The main cause of toxoplasma infection is eating tissue cysts in raw or undercooked meat, poultry or seafood. So ensure all meat is thoroughly cooked before eating. Avoid processed meats such as salami or ham.

- ❖ Fruit and vegetables should be peeled or thoroughly washed before eating, even if you have grown them (organically) yourself. Salads should be washed too.

- ❖ Wash hands, knives, chopping boards, dishes, counters and utensils with hot soapy water after they have been in contact with raw meat, poultry, seafood or unwashed fruit and vegetables. Ideally, wear gloves when handling raw meat (including raw meat that may be fed to cats or other pets) and remove them before handling other foodstuffs.

- ❖ Do not consume any milk or milk products that are unpasteurised; this includes milk (especially goat's milk), colostrum and any other dairy product. Cook all eggs before consumption.

- ❖ Wear gloves when gardening, as cats may have used your garden as a toilet. Wash your hands and nails thoroughly after gardening. Cover children's sandpits or boxes to discourage cats from using them as a toilet.

- ❖ Good hygiene during pregnancy can decrease the frequency of toxoplasma infection by almost two-thirds. Always wash hands thoroughly after contact with pets or farm animals as well as their faeces or environments.

- ❖ Get advice from your doctor if you are planning an overseas trip.

> **Ensure all meat is thoroughly cooked before eating**

Should I get rid of my cat?

Remember, you are at no greater risk of contracting toxoplasmosis if you own a cat. Simple precautions reduce the risk. Infection with toxoplasma via the environment or uncooked meat is much more common than infection directly from cats.

If anyone suggests rehoming your cat, then discuss your individual risk profile with your doctor. And show them this book!

> **You are at no greater risk of contracting toxoplasmosis if you own a cat**

What should I do?

While it can be easy to let fears and worries mount when you are expecting, don't add toxoplasmosis to your list. As long as you are practising safe and hygienic behaviour in the garden, before handling food, and after emptying your cat's litter box each day, your risk of catching toxoplasma from your cat is minimal.

Don't suddenly move your indoor cat outdoors; this increases the chance that they will get toxoplasma from hunting birds and animals and then shed eggs in their faeces.

Remember, no direct correlation has been found between cat ownership and human toxoplasma infection, whereas consuming raw or undercooked meat significantly increases the risk of acquiring this infection. In saying this, though, the chance of catching toxoplasmosis during pregnancy is very low in developed countries.

Toxoplasmosis in cats

Cats become infected with *Toxoplasma gondii* when they eat raw meat or catch and eat infected prey such as rats, mice and birds or, more rarely, by ingesting flies, soil, or water contaminated with eggs from cat faeces.

What are the symptoms?

Most healthy cats will show so few symptoms that you won't know they have been infected. If cats do show symptoms, these usually include fever, decreased appetite, lethargy and possibly diarrhoea. Rarely, more serious cases may develop into pneumonia, eye and neurological problems.

When cats first contract toxoplasmosis, they begin shedding millions of eggs in their faeces for about one to three weeks, making both the faeces and wherever it is deposited infective to humans and other animals. They may shed again in the future, although this is rare and involves fewer eggs.

Can I test my cat for it?

Diagnostic tests are sometimes recommended to try to determine if your cat is shedding eggs.

Blood tests measure the antibodies in a cat's blood, and help determine if there are eggs in the cat's faeces. An antibody-positive cat is unlikely to be currently shedding eggs and is unlikely to shed in the future, and is therefore of less risk to a human's health. An antibody-negative cat is potentially shedding or will shed eggs for one to three weeks in the future, if exposed for the first time. This cat poses a higher risk to a human's health.

Faecal tests are not particularly accurate and are only useful if eggs are detected in the faeces. If they are, this indicates that the cat will shed for another one to three weeks and then stop (though in rare cases they may re-shed in future).

In summary, no test accurately guarantees that your cat is not shedding or will not shed eggs in the future. All cats in a household with a pregnant woman should be treated in the same way regardless of test results. With simple precautions and basic hygiene, the risk of contracting toxoplasmosis from your cat is minimal. See **www.babyandpet.com.au** for more detailed information and if you are still concerned then discuss this with your veterinarian.

The wrong suspect

Expectant parents Tina and Jay came to visit me with Rolly, their beloved eight-year-old Burmese. They were enquiring about finding a new home for him. Rolly certainly didn't like visiting the clinic – I always need a nurse to assist me in keeping his claws out of my skin while examining him.

I assumed that he was just as aggressive at home and their concern was that he might scratch their baby. How wrong I was – Rolly was an angel at home, they told me, and their issue was something much more upsetting.

Tina and Jay had been trying to conceive for many years and had experienced numerous fertility treatments and IVF procedures. Finally, what seemed like a miracle had occurred and Tina was now pregnant. Upon announcing the good news, their fertility doctor told them to 'get rid of the cat' as it was not 'worth the risk of toxoplasmosis' after their struggle to conceive. Understandably, Tina and Jay were very distressed about the thought of giving up Rolly, but they were reluctant to go against their doctor's advice.

Tina told me that she'd had a specific blood test for toxoplasma a few months before her pregnancy. This blood test had shown that she had never contracted toxoplasma, despite having owned and cared for Rolly for eight years. The good news for her was that, if she had not contracted toxoplasma in the last eight years from Rolly, then it was extremely unlikely that she would catch it from him in the next nine months while pregnant.

They were surprised when I told them that they were much more likely to catch toxoplasma from undercooked meat or from gardening than from their pampered indoor-dwelling feline.

I gave them my notes about toxoplasma, which are now this chapter of *Tell Your Cat You're Pregnant*, and told them to go home and read them carefully.

A week later, Tina rang to thank me: my advice had allayed her fears. Jay was cleaning the litter tray daily, and Tina had implemented stricter hygiene and cooking procedures. She had shown the fertility doctor the information I had given her in the hope that he would update his advice.

Nearly a year later, Tina visited me again for Rolly's booster vaccination. She had a big smile on her face, pushing a healthy baby, Ethan, in his pram, and with a hissing and spitting Rolly in his carrier. I can't say I was delighted to see Rolly that day, but I was thrilled that he was still a member of the family.

4
Aggression

The chance of your household cat being aggressive or injuring your baby is low; but any aggression by cats directed towards babies or children is a concern. Not only can their teeth and claws do damage, they can also transmit bacterial infections to humans (for example, cat scratch disease – see Chapter 9: Staying healthy).

Identifying the cause of aggression (biting or scratching) in cats can be difficult. There may not be one clear reason. Many owners of aggressive cats say they just lash out or attack for no apparent reason. It is only after a thorough assessment by a person experienced in cat behaviour that the true cause of the aggression can be determined.

If your cat has been aggressive towards people or animals in the past, you need to consult an appropriate veterinarian immediately. It is best to work on these issues well before the arrival of a baby.

For cats that may be aggressive, training them to wear a harness or go into a cat carrier on command may be helpful (see Chapter 8).

Techniques such as yelling, loud clapping or hitting do not work with cats and may cause fear aggression. Punishment also makes cats anxious, and anxiety reduces a cat's ability to learn, especially to learn about positive associations. A cat will learn to associate pain or fear with punishment and eventually the association can develop into outright aggression. Obviously this is not the harmonious family relationship you desire, so never use verbal or physical punishment with your cat.

> Never use verbal or physical
> punishment with your cat

Cats can remain agitated for long periods, so it is important to keep them safely and securely separated in an area away from people for a period once they are aggressive or appear annoyed (that is, behaviour group C — see Chapter 6: Knowing your cat). Some cats can even take several days to calm down after an aggressive incident so ensure you allow them adequate time in this area to calm down. Be careful not to pick them up when relocating them to this area if they are aggressive as they could injure you. If they are not trained on a harness or responding to your cues to go into their safe haven, use a thick blanket, cardboard or cushions, etc. to protect yourself and shepherd them into this area.

Learned aggression

Cats can learn that acts of aggression will give them a desired result. For example, some cats can become aggressive towards their owners when they want to be fed and the food is delayed. The cat then bites the owner because they are irritable and so, naturally, the owner feeds them to stop the biting. The cat then learns that biting their owner means they will be fed.

Fear or defensive aggression

Cat aggression towards newborns is not usually associated with jealousy, or with being 'put out', or with an urge to dominate. Depending on early experiences, previous contact with babies or individual temperaments, many cats fear babies and the noises or movements they make. This fear can be seen as either cats hiding from babies or sometimes as aggression.

**Many cats are scared of babies
and the noises they make**

In some cats there is a learned component to the fear aggression. Often a cat may initially be fearful of a person and show body postures associated with fear that go unrecognised. Over time they may start to use aggression to help them to maintain distance from the person they fear. Then this fear aggression may become pre-emptive (instead of reactionary) and the cat may appear to attack the person 'without reason', when in fact the underlying initial cause for the aggression is fear. It is vital that the cat does not learn that aggression is its only option, since eventually the cat could respond aggressively to anyone.

A fearful cat will first try to escape, but if they are pursued or cannot escape they may fluff out their coat, hiss, spit and arch their back and

paw at anyone who approaches (that is, behaviour group C — see Chapter 6: Knowing your cat). If the person continues the pursuit, the cat may lash out. This is fearful or defensive aggression. Children cannot recognise these warning behaviour signs, so it is important that all interactions between cats and children are supervised (see Chapter 8: Supervising, separating and training). Any cornered animal may attack.

> **Young children do not understand cat body language**

Lack of socialisation

Studies have shown that cats that have been inadequately socialised or handled by people (including children) before around three months of age are more fearful and aggressive to people regardless of the circumstances. Such cats do not voluntarily approach people and are aggressive if they cannot escape. If this is your cat then you need to seek the assistance of an appropriate veterinarian.

Aggression due to pain or illness

Any illness or painful condition can make a cat act aggressively. Cats can also hold a memory of past pain long after the old injury has healed, and they may continue to dislike being touched in this area, for example, if they have had skin or ear complaints. In older cats, an overactive thyroid, arthritis or dental issues can also result in aggression. Any illness in your cat should be promptly addressed by your veterinarian.

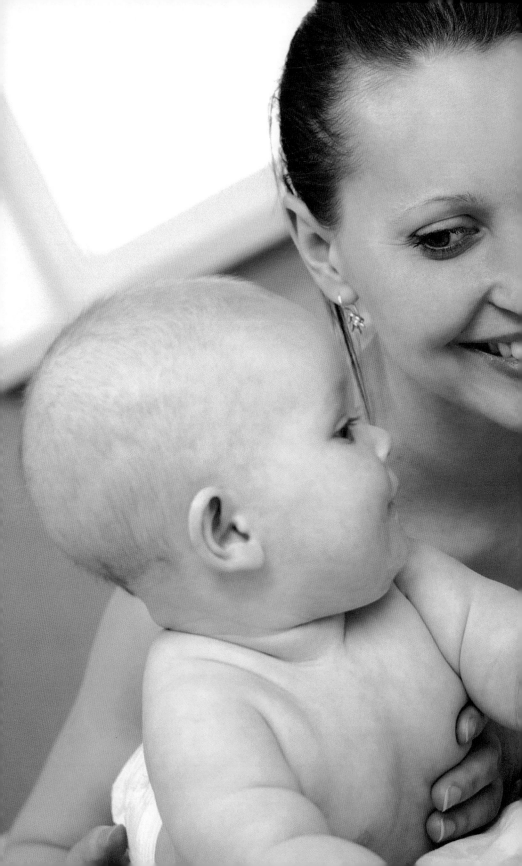

All interactions between cats and children should be supervised

Territorial aggression

Cats can be territorially aggressive, especially towards other cats that encroach on their space. Some cats may also be territorially aggressive towards people and potentially a new baby in the house. This would appear as aggression directed towards the baby when you first arrive home. Thankfully few cats display this, and generally there are warning signs (for example, your cat might have attacked new visitors in the past). If this is your cat, then you need to seek the advice of an appropriate veterinarian.

Play aggression

Play aggression is a normal behaviour in kittens. As they grow older they learn to direct this aggression only towards inanimate objects or toys (that is, behaviour group D — see Chapter 6: Knowing your cat). Often kittens are encouraged by owners to scratch, bite and play with their owners' hands or feet. When doing this, kittens can learn to scratch and bite hard. Often owners consider this type of play cute and harmless when the cat is young, but when the cat has full-sized teeth and claws it is suddenly painful and considered aggressive. However, the cat may still see it all as just play. Often if techniques such as yelling, pushing or smacking are then incorrectly used by owners to try to stop this behaviour, this can cause the cat to now become fearfully aggressive (see above). If your cat is accustomed to mouthing and scratching your hands, now is the time to teach them to play with toys attached to strings or other toys, rather than skin, so that they will know not to use their mouth or claws when interacting with the baby.

> **Do not punish your cat for showing play aggression**

A cat expressing play aggression may stalk you, or hide somewhere and jump out, or vocalise and attack you as you pass. Do not punish your cat for this behaviour, especially not physically, but try ignoring them, so that the play aggression is not rewarded with attention. This may mean wearing thick jeans or boots inside the house so that you do not respond when they grab you. You can also drag a toy attached to a piece of string around with you for them to attack, rather than your legs/feet. Putting a bell on your cat's collar can help foil their sneak attacks. If this aggression continues, seek advice from an appropriate veterinarian.

Cats chasing a toy on a string or similar object can easily pounce on and scratch a baby if the toy comes too close to the baby. For this reason it is best not to play with toys near a baby on the floor. Rather, use toys you can throw, such as ping-pong balls or scrunched-up paper, and save string toys for when baby is somewhere safe. Encourage more gentle activities when the baby is present and more vigorous activities when the baby is absent. Over time this may help to teach the cat that vigorous play should not occur near the baby.

The playful kitten

I could see the problem John and Gillian were having with their ten-month-old kitten, Toby, before I even met him. Both John's and Gillian's arms were covered in lots of tiny scratches. 'He's mauling us to pieces!' said Gillian half-jokingly. 'His claws and teeth are just so sharp! We need your help. I am worried for our unborn baby,' she continued more seriously.

John and Gillian had adopted Toby from a shelter at about three months of age. He was a delightful kitten and was perfect in every way, except that, whenever they went to pet him or pick him up, he would latch onto their hands with his teeth and scratch them with his claws. He would also chase and attack their ankles and legs as they walked around the house. They were worried that this aggression would injure their baby.

Gillian showed me some gorgeous photos of Toby as a kitten as she described how they played with him when he was young. When he first arrived home, John and Gillian both loved nothing more than wrestling, playing and 'attacking' Toby with their hands and feet, encouraging him to attack them back in a playful manner. At that young age, his teeth and claws did not hurt. Now he was bigger, his claws and teeth where much stronger and John and Gillian were no longer enjoying this type of play. I explained to them that Toby was showing play aggression and, despite his owners' pain, he saw all these interactions as great fun.

John had been researching possible treatment options on the internet, so we first discussed the use of inappropriate techniques such as yelling or tapping Toby on the nose when he was being aggressive. I told them that these techniques are *not* recommended as they can cause a playful cat to become fearful of their owner. Sometimes this can progress to fear aggression, which is much more serious, especially with a new baby in the house.

From now on all play with hands or feet was to stop. If Toby did start to play aggressively with their hands or feet, they were to stop moving that body part and either wait for Toby to lose interest and detach or distract him from them by throwing a toy.

I instructed John and Gillian to increase the amount of Toby's vigorous playtime with toys at a distance from them. This included: balls to be thrown; feathers or toys on a string attached to a stick; or pretend mice; and any other games *not* associated with hands or feet that Toby enjoyed playing. This vigorous play was to be performed for 20 minutes at least twice daily. If they wanted to play rough with Toby they were to use a large rope toy for him to sink his teeth and claws into – never their bare hands or feet.

When walking around the house with bare feet and ankles, they were to drag a toy on a string behind them or throw a toy that Toby liked to chase to distract him from attacking their legs. At other times they were to wear thick boots and jeans and stop moving if Toby latched onto their ankle. They were then to wait until he lost interest or distract him away with a toy.

Three months later I bumped into John at the supermarket. The first thing I noticed was the lack of scratches on his arms, and I knew before even asking him that Toby was a changed man.

Predatory aggression

Predatory aggression is a normal instinctive desire to hunt prey, and includes the stalking, chasing and attacking of small mammals and birds (that is, behaviour group D — see Chapter 6: Knowing your cat). However, this behaviour is inappropriate when directed towards people — especially infants and toddlers, who may be vulnerable to predatory aggression.

As discussed in 'Play aggression' above, some cats like to hide, stalk and pounce on their owners when they are walking around the house. Often this is when their owners are at their most vulnerable (that is, naked). For most cats this is play, but if your cat is silent when they pounce then this indicates it is more likely to be displaying predatory behaviour and your cat perceives you as an object to hunt and 'kill'. Play aggression is usually associated with vocalisation, but distinguishing between play and predatory aggression can be difficult. Both types of behaviour, whether play or predatory, can be quite serious with a baby in the house and you should seek advice from an appropriate veterinarian if your cat is behaving in this way.

Petting-induced aggression

Petting-induced aggression – when your cat suddenly becomes aggressive while you are petting them – can be caused by overstimulation or by petting your cat beyond their tolerance. It can also happen when you stroke areas of your cat's body that they don't like to be touched (for example, their belly).

Early signs your cat may show before becoming aggressive are:

- ❖ suddenly freezing
- ❖ staring at the hand that is touching them
- ❖ leaning away or shifting body position
- ❖ dilating their pupils

- flicking their tail
- flexing/unsheathing their claws
- rippling/twitching fur along their back
- tensing their body
- flattening/twitching ears
- ceasing to purr and starting to growl or meow.

Pay attention to your cat's body language

When you first notice any of these signs in your cat, stop touching them. You might even need to encourage your cat to jump off your lap, stand up so they drop off your lap, or simply move away from the cat and allow them to calm down. Young children are unable to interpret a cat's body language, exposing them to greater risk of a scratch or bite injury while petting.

To avoid petting-induced aggression, pay attention to your cat's body language and learn their tolerance level so you can stay well below that when you pet them. For example, they may only enjoy being stroked on the head. The hardest part of owning a cat that displays petting-induced aggression is accepting that your cat may not be a 'cuddly cat' and that there are limits to what they will tolerate. Some cats prefer to interact with their owners in ways other than being petted or cuddled (for example, playing with a toy on a string) and it is important to respect this.

You can attempt to increase the level of your cat's tolerance to petting by offering them tasty treats while they are being petted. Monitor their body language though, and stop petting if they show any of the above signs; reward your cat when they allow petting without showing these signs. Gradually increase the length of petting time, while offering rewards, over a period of weeks to months.

Milo the tiger

'Milo is like a tiger!' Kylie said. 'He is attacking me and my husband without warning and his teeth and claws are sharp!' Kylie was five months pregnant and she was, naturally, concerned that Milo would attack and injure their new baby.

I scheduled a house call to see if I could tame the 'tiger'.

When I arrived at the house, I rang the doorbell with some trepidation, then a man I guessed must be Kylie's husband, Tony, opened the door and beckoned me to enter the living area to meet Kylie and Milo the tiger.

As I sat on the couch, a gorgeous two-year-old fluffy Birman cat jumped onto my lap, made himself comfortable and started purring – this was Milo. It looked like Milo wouldn't hurt a flea. As I was absent-mindedly petting him while we humans chatted about the problem, I noticed his tail start to flick and his pupils dilate slightly and, just in time, I stopped petting him, stood up and let him drop off my lap. His teeth and claws just missed me as he fell and ran under the couch. His owners were amazed that I had avoided being scratched or bitten. They truly thought I was a cat whisperer who was going to tame their 'tiger'.

Milo accepted petting for a certain period, but then would suddenly lash out and attack his owners. He would not show aggression at any other time – only when being petted. I discussed 'petting-induced aggression' with them and how some cats have a limited tolerance for being petted. We also discussed the body language that he was showing when he was becoming agitated. They were amazed they had not noticed these signs.

As the aggression only occurred when Milo was being petted, we discussed how unlikely he was to cause injury to their baby. It might become a problem if they were cuddling their baby and petting Milo at the same time, or when their baby was old enough to pet Milo. It was crucial for them to ensure they provided adequate supervision or separation to avoid injury. This provided much reassurance that their Milo could be tamed.

Redirected aggression

This is when your cat sees something they want to attack (for example, another cat), usually through a window, but because they cannot attack it, your cat attacks whatever is nearby – a person or another pet, or possibly your baby.

It's easy to misunderstand redirected aggression because you may miss whatever is upsetting your cat. Even though the initial incident may have happened some time ago, your cat may still respond aggressively. When an incident of redirected aggression occurs between previously friendly cats they may remain hostile towards each other long after whatever triggered the redirected aggression has passed, especially if it was severe.

Sibling rivalry

Cats fighting within a household are a serious concern if you are expecting a baby. A baby could easily be injured through redirected aggression or if cats are fighting nearby. Take care when breaking up a cat fight: owners are frequently injured when attempting to do this. If your cats are involved in aggressive incidents then you need to seek the assistance of an appropriate veterinarian.

5
Toileting issues

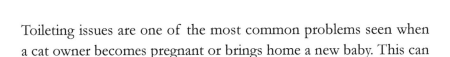

Toileting issues are one of the most common problems seen when a cat owner becomes pregnant or brings home a new baby. This can be divided into:

* toileting outside the litter box (that is, urine and sometimes faeces – anywhere around the house); or
* urine spraying or marking.

> **Toileting issues commonly occur with the arrival of a new baby**

Toileting issues can be frustrating and complex to treat. Despite this, some simple solutions are discussed below. Be aware that the longer your cat has had a toileting issue, the harder it is to treat, so seek timely advice from an appropriate veterinarian if these remedies do not appear to be working. Punishment (for example, yelling, locking your cat away or spraying water at your cat) is not recommended as it often leads to your cat learning to toilet in your absence or in an area that you do not notice. Punishment will also increase your cat's anxiety and potentially worsen the problem.

There can be medical causes for any toileting issue, so your cat *must* be checked by your veterinarian first if they are showing signs of toileting problems. In male cats, their urinary tract can become blocked, which means they are unable to urinate. This is an emergency.

If your male cat is straining to go to the toilet, but not passing any urine (or only small amounts) then you need to visit your veterinarian immediately. Once medical causes have been ruled out or treated, then the behavioural aspects of the toileting issues can be addressed.

> There can be medical cause
> for toileting issues

Toileting outside the litter box

This is where your cat starts going to the toilet (that is, urinating and sometimes defecating) in areas other than the litter box. It may be right next to the box or in a totally different place inside the house such as in the bathtub or shower, on clothes, carpet or sometimes even on an owner's bed or the baby's new mattress! Your cat may show a preference for toileting on a particular substance or in a particular location and use the litter box infrequently or not at all. Some cats may still use the box for faeces only and urinate elsewhere. This is different to urine spraying/marking (see below).

Toileting outside the litter box usually means your cat:

❖ dislikes the litter box or the litter or both; and/or
❖ prefers a different location or substance to go to the toilet on.

When an owner is pregnant or a baby arrives home, some of the common reasons your cat may start toileting outside the litter box are:

❖ a change in your routine (for example, less time to clean the litter box);
❖ a sudden relocation of the litter box;

❖   the litter box is no longer in a place that suits your cat (for example, in close proximity to a noisy washing machine/drier that is being used more often to wash the baby's clothes).

Some cats may identify the litter box with unpleasant experiences (for example, pain from bladder issues, constipation or arthritis; being captured there and taken off to the vet; or feeling exposed or unsafe). Other cats dislike the litter so much that they go in search of something more pleasant on which to toilet. It can be difficult to establish the reasons behind toileting outside the litter box, so you may need to seek advice from an appropriate veterinarian.

Treatment

Many of the treatment suggestions for toileting outside the litter box will also assist with urine spraying/marking (see below).

Your aim is to make the litter box and its location more attractive and the toileting place(s) outside the litter box less attractive. To work out what is causing the problem, ideally change only one aspect of the litter box at a time.

> **Make the litter box more attractive for your cat**

Litter box specifications

❖   Change the type of litter. Many cats prefer fine, sandy, clumping litters.
❖   Buy a litter that contains activated carbon, if available, to absorb smells.

❖ Make sure the litter is 5 cm (2 inches) deep.

❖ Cover or uncover the litter box to suit your cat's preferences. Covered litter boxes not only trap odours but may also make it difficult for a cat to see the approach of other pets, which can discourage them from using the box.

❖ Increase the size of the litter box. Larger boxes (for example, plastic office-storage or sweater boxes) are more appealing to cats than typical boxes sold as 'litter boxes' by pet stores. Ensure your cat can get in and out easily, especially if they are arthritic.

Litter box location

❖ Place a litter box over the soiled area being used by your cat. If they start to use it, then very gradually move the litter box, a couple of inches daily, until it is in an area that is more socially acceptable.

❖ Provide one litter box per cat and one extra. Provide at least one litter box on each level of your house and make sure litter boxes are not visible from each other.

❖ The litter box ideally should be located in a quiet area where the cat is unlikely to be disturbed by sudden noises, people or animals, or a crawling baby. Avoid areas near noisy washing machines, dryers or refrigerators and also areas with a lot of human traffic. If you have two or more cats, try to ensure that one of your cats cannot prevent the other from accessing the litter box or ambush it when it is using or leaving the toileting area. Provide several entry and exit points to enable the cat to avoid these issues. When your child is mobile, make sure they cannot disturb the cat while they are toileting. No one likes to be disturbed on the toilet, although new parents have to forgo that privilege for a few years!

Deter toileting in locations other than the litter box

❖ Restrict your cat's access to areas where the toileting issues occur (for example, close doors or place furniture over the area).

❖ Use enzymatic odour eliminators to clean up the urine in the soiled areas. Avoid ammonia-based cleaning products, which can attract cats to urinate.

❖ Deterrents may also be helpful. Consider citrus sprays or scents, aluminium foil, inverted plastic carpet runners, double-sided sticky tape, sandpaper, thick plastic sheets, bubble wrap, trays of marbles, or anything else that will prevent your cat from accessing the inappropriate area where they have been toileting.

❖ If your cat toilets in the bathtub or shower, leave a few inches of water in the bottom as a deterrent. However, ensure that this is not a drowning hazard for your baby.

❖ Most cats will not defecate where they eat or play. Try feeding your cat in the spot where they toilet inappropriately. Dry cat food may work best because it takes longer to eat. Sometimes gluing a few pieces of dried cat food to an old saucer or piece of cardboard and placing it in the soiled location can deter some cats.

❖ Place the cat's bedding, toys, cat tree or scratching post in the place they toilet.

Litter box appeal

❖ Make the litter box more appealing to your cat.

❖ Provide a range of litters and litter boxes and note which one the cat prefers. Place it in the current soiled area.

❖ Change from scented to unscented litter or vice versa.

❖ Avoid deodorisers in or around litter boxes – these products may smell nice to us, but they are often a deterrent to your cat!

Litter box cleaning

❖ Many cats will not use a dirty litter box, so discard all litter box contents and wash the box with hot soapy water daily (see Chapter 3: Toxoplasmosis). Don't use disinfectants or cleaners or heavily scented products. Rinse well and air dry. If it is hard to remove the smell from an old litter box, replace it.

❖ Self-cleaning litter boxes may be convenient, but your cat may not like the sound or movement they make.

A feline thank you

Mark and Peta had a smelly problem with Tigger, their Ragdoll cat. He had started using the ensuite bath as his toilet. He usually did this early in the morning, so Mark and Peta were woken by the terrible smell. Tigger's problem worried his owners even more as he was using the bath for faeces but still urinating normally in his litter box. Also, Peta was almost nine months pregnant and soon the bath would be used for their baby. His regular veterinarian had declared Tigger healthy after a recent examination and now they approached me for behavioural advice.

I toured the house with Mark and Peta, taking note of the litter box location, feeding stations and other issues that might be causing the problem. The couple were worried that Tigger might be anxious about the pending arrival. They also thought it might be a form of protest, as it had started around the time Mark began a new job and was frequently away from home.

As we discussed things further, it became apparent that the problem was related to Mark's new job – but not in the way his owners suspected. When Peta was newly pregnant, Mark had taken over the duties of cleaning the litter box daily. But since starting his new job he would often be away for several days in a row and the litter box would not be emptied during this time. My suspicion was that Tigger liked his toilet to be fastidiously clean and he was using the bath as an alternate toileting location when he found the litter box unacceptable.

As both owners could share litter-box-cleaning duties once their baby was born, we discussed in the meantime placing an extra litter box in the ensuite that Tigger could use if the original box was dirty. This should stop him from using the bath. Once their baby was born this litter box could then be removed. I also suggested filling the bath with an inch of water to deter Tigger from toileting in there.

As I was leaving, Mark had a further comment – Tigger often used the litter box as soon as Mark cleaned it out. This was frustrating, as he would then have to immediately clean it again. I told him this was Tigger's way of saying, 'Thank you for cleaning my toilet'. I'm not sure Mark enjoyed the joke …

Urine spraying

Urine spraying or marking is when your cat backs up to something and 'sprays' it with small amounts of urine. It is usually a vertical surface (for example, a wall or curtain). Urine spraying is a common problem when cats are anxious or stressed, which might happen when there are changes in the house such as preparations for a new baby, as well as the actual arrival of the baby. Urine spraying is a normal way for cats to communicate; unfortunately, some cats are more 'communicative' when they are stressed or anxious.

> **Urine spraying can occur when a cat is anxious or stressed**

Areas urinated on usually have a special social or behavioural significance (for example, baby clothes, new furniture or door and window frames); they are usually ideal places to send messages to other cats who might be planning to enter the house. Often a spraying cat will use the litter box normally for urine and faeces the rest of the time.

Both male and female cats can spray, even if they have been neutered. If you keep in mind that urine spraying is a means of communication, your cat's behaviour may be easier to understand. While humans may manage their own anxiety by talking about the problem, cats may deal with their anxiety by spraying, even though they appear to be totally normal in the rest of their behaviour.

Treatment

All of the treatments discussed under the heading 'Toileting outside the litter box' above will also assist with urine spraying, but there are additional measures to try too:

- ❖ Neutering male and female cats has been shown to cause a decrease in spraying.
- ❖ Do not clean corners around the house that are at head height for your cat. These are likely to have been rubbed by your cat (facial marking) and a pheromone left there, which can lower anxiety for some cats.
- ❖ Decrease any obvious causes of anxiety (apart from removing your baby!). Environmental enrichment is an important part of anxiety reduction and should be increased for these cats (see Chapter 10: Preparing your cat).
- ❖ Spray Feliway directly on the marked areas, or use a Feliway diffuser, or both (see 'Feliway' in Chapter 9: Staying healthy).
- ❖ Medications that lower anxiety can be helpful for spraying cats, so consult your veterinarian.

Sox the stress-head

When I walked into Carolyn and Mike's house, I immediately knew what the problem was with their cat, Sox. The pungent odour of cat urine was thick in the air. They told me that Sox was not coping with the arrival of baby Liam and had begun urinating in prominent areas around the house almost as soon as Liam arrived home. Carolyn and Mike were frustrated – they wanted to enjoy time with their precious newborn but Sox was making their home rather unpleasant. Naturally, they were concerned that Sox didn't like Liam and was taking it out on them by urinating around the house.

After discussions with Carolyn and Mike, it seemed that there had been a lot of changes to Sox's environment at the same time as Liam's arrival. On the day Liam arrived home they had to move Sox's litter box and food and water bowls to more suitable locations. Previously, Mike used to play regularly with Sox when he came home from work, and Carolyn also used to interact with Sox in the morning before she left for work. Now that Liam was around, these times had sadly, but perhaps understandably, disappeared. Furthermore, Sox used to enjoy lounging on the window seat in the nursery

for large portions of the day. Now he had been excluded from the nursery, as Mike and Carolyn did not think he should be in there.

These were clearly some big changes for Sox in a short period of time. Changes such as these often cause cats to become stressed and, judging from the locations of urine around the house, it was obvious to me that Sox was urine spraying. Urine spraying is often caused by stress or anxiety. The sudden changes in Sox's environment were clearly the cause for his spraying, and not the arrival of Liam. After explaining this to Mike and Carolyn, they were very relieved. I reassured them that Liam and Sox could be best friends.

Managing Sox's stress would help to decrease his urine spraying. Carolyn and Mike needed to initially reverse some of the changes that had been made to Sox's household routine. We discussed allowing Sox access to the window seat in the nursery when they were present or when Liam was not in the nursery. In the nursery, we also installed an elevated perch-style scratching post next to the change table to enable Sox to be near his owners while they tended to Liam. Both owners vowed to reintroduce some dedicated times with Sox at least twice daily. We installed a pheromone diffuser to help with Sox's anxiety and I recommended a short course of anxiety-lowering medication to help Sox cope with the stressful transition. We also discussed how best to clean the urine and make some of the urine-marked areas inaccessible to him. Mike and Carolyn also implemented some environmental enrichment in the form of elevated resting places and hidey-holes to help with Sox's stress.

Four months later I dropped in to check how Sox was going. He was much more relaxed with the situation now. He still occasionally urine sprayed when a new item was brought into the home or there was a major change to his routine, but Mike and Carolyn were much more aware of this. They learnt to gradually introduce any changes into the house so as not to stress him. I must say, their house now smelt a lot nicer, too!

6

Knowing your cat

A well-prepared cat is more likely to accept a new baby without problems. The first step is to know your cat and how they are likely to react to something new and strange. The next step is to prepare your cat carefully, and well in advance, for the arrival of your new baby.

> **Prepare your cat well in advance for a new baby**

Assessing your cat's body language

There are many subtle variations in feline body language. Outlined below are some signs to watch for that will assist you in assessing your cat's mood. Some are obvious; others are subtle. These signs are collected into behaviour groups A, B, C and D, to give you a general appreciation of your cat's emotional state. This is especially helpful when you come to play the baby and toy sounds – you should be able to identify your cat's reaction. The behaviour groups can also be used to assess your cat's emotional state in other situations.

Assessment based purely on these behaviour groups is not a substitute for seeking professional advice. If you are having trouble assessing your cat's behavioural signs then seek help from an appropriate veterinarian.

Reading your cat's body language

You need to be able to read your cat's body language to understand how they are feeling. To do this, watch your cat closely in many different situations and observe their body language. For example, do they hiss, cower and hide when visitors arrive, or rub up against them with their tail held high? At all times when assessing your cat, try to put yourself in their shoes (or paws). Try to determine if your cat is comfortable and relaxed. Trust your instincts; you know your cat. If something does not feel right about your cat's behaviour, either towards the baby sounds or towards your baby, then it probably isn't right. It is better to seek professional advice from an appropriate veterinarian and be sure than to be sorry later. Never force a cat to interact if they do not want to.

By understanding body language and posture, it is possible to tell a cat's mood even when they are not close to you. Cat's facial signals, however, are more subtle and change more quickly, providing a more immediate indication of how your cat is feeling.

> **You can often tell a cat's mood by reading their body language**

Try to consider your cat as a whole; looking at just one body part gives you only a small piece of the picture. Body language in cats is variable and can depend on the individual cat, and some behaviours can fit into multiple categories.

If your cat displays any concerning behaviour, such as growling, hissing or questionable body language (see behaviour groups B, C and D below) during any interaction with the baby (or the baby doll – see below), never punish it. Your cat is letting you know they are uncomfortable, and they are communicating in a normal, natural and appropriate manner. Yelling at or correcting your cat will not make

them adjust faster or better. In fact, you may be teaching your cat that giving you a warning is a bad thing, and next time your cat may skip the warning and go straight to aggression. Warnings are helpful and tell you that your cat is not comfortable and that you need to remove them from the situation. If the signs persist, you will need to seek assistance from an appropriate veterinarian.

Additionally, just because your cat reacted undesirably to your baby or child does not necessarily mean you need to give your cat away; this may be an issue that can be remedied. Contact an appropriate veterinarian immediately. Never attempt to deal with aggression or questionable behaviour on your own. Remember, understanding when a cat might attack can save you from injury.

> **If your cat is aggressive seek help from an appropriate veterinarian**

Eyes

Look into your cat's eyes. You can tell a lot from their pupils. They expand and contract depending on how your cat is feeling. If they are little more than slits, your cat is probably calm and content. When they are widely dilated, your cat is probably fearful. The greater the threat, the larger the pupils. However, the size of the pupil alone is insufficient when judging your cat's emotional state as pupil size can also change according to the ambient light, arousal, excitement or aggression. If you see your cat's pupils change in response to your behaviour ... stop! Evaluate the environment and your behaviour. If the pupil returns to normal, you know the situation has improved.

Relaxed, contented and calm cats will often show relaxed, heavy-lidded, slow eye blinks. Sometimes mimicking your cat with these blinks may encourage them to blink back at you. Some owners call this a 'cat kiss'.

Cat's eyes have a black pupil and a coloured iris (see the picture above).

If your cat avoids eye contact or looks away, they are trying to avoid conflict by refusing to interact with you.

Direct eye contact combined with attention-seeking behaviour often means your cat is trying to persuade you to hand over something they want.

A cat that gives you a hard, unblinking stare with dilated pupils, and leans forward, holding themselves still, could be issuing a challenge or a threat. Staring can often be intimidating.

If your cat's eyes are tightly shut, it could mean they have shut down, are highly stressed or are blocking external stimuli. Your cat is not asleep — they are shutting out the environment.

Ears

Your cat's ears can move in all directions and independently of each other. These movements tell you a lot about how your cat is feeling.

Erect ears mean your cat is alert. Flicking ears means irritation. If their ears stick out sideways they are on the defensive, feeling annoyed or fearful. The flatter the ears the more aggressive they are likely to be — it is best to leave this cat alone or serious injury may occur.

Tail

A cat's tail can express a wide range of emotions. Cats are usually very precise in their tail placement and often deliberately touch objects, people and other animals with their tails as they walk around.

> **A cat's tail can express a wide range of emotions**

A tail held up vertically as a cat walks, or wrapped around the body as they sit or lie, signals relaxed, friendly intentions. An unusually fluffed-up tail and/or fur along their back indicates fear.

Tail flicking or twitching can mean an agitated, annoyed or aroused cat, and the faster and bigger the flicks the more agitated the cat. Failure to notice this signal can cause a cat to become aggressive.

Whiskers

A relaxed cat has whiskers sticking out sideways or in a neutral position. Whiskers pointing backwards show your cat would like some space. If they are held forward, your cat may be gathering information. They may be curious or preparing to attack and you will need to assess the rest of their body language to obtain further information.

Body

Body posture alone can be a poor indicator of your cat's current mood. Often you will need to assess other signs to identify your cat's true emotional state.

Voice

Cats are vocal creatures capable of making a wide range of different sounds. Hissing is a warning signal to keep your distance. Often a cat hisses when they feel cornered and unable to escape.

Purring is usually the sign of a happy cat, although some cats will purr when in pain. A cat in pain will usually also have dilated pupils and show agitated body language.

Panting

Cats do not normally pant as dogs do. If a cat is panting it is usually a sign of extreme fear, anxiety, pain, illness, overexertion or overheating. A highly stressed cat will also sweat through the pads of their feet and shed fur.

Fur

The higher your cat's fur sticks up the more intense is your cat's emotional response. This can be fear, aggression or arousal. Twitching or rolling of the skin and fur can indicate irritation or pain.

Pheromones

Pheromones are special substances produced by your cat that provide information to other cats but also to themselves. They are made in glands found on their face, between their toes and at the base of their tail. Many of your cat's most appealing actions, such as rubbing their head or cheek against you (bunting), or winding around your ankles, are actually ways of marking you with familiarisation pheromones. Cats may bunt or rub against a baby or new item in the house to put a familiar scent on these strange new presences in their territory.

Do not clean furniture or objects your cat has rubbed or bunted on as this may remove their familiarisation scent. Any disturbance in the scent profile of your cat's territory could increase their anxiety. Feliway is a commercially available synthetic copy of this pheromone and can be applied to new baby items (for example, strollers, cots or cribs and highchairs) to make them smell more familiar and less threatening (see 'Feliway' in Chapter 9: Staying healthy).

Behaviour groups

Each of the four behaviour groups outlined below contains behaviours that will help you assess how your cat is feeling. These groupings are by no means exhaustive. Every cat has its own individual body language and its own behavioural responses. The signs should only be used as a guide to your cat's current emotional state. You can use the behaviour group signs to assess your cat in *any* situation – not just when you are playing the baby and toy sounds to familiarise your cat to the noises they may hear when your baby arrives.

> **Use the behaviours groups to assess your cat in any situation**

Behaviour group A

Your cat may exhibit *one or more* of these signs, indicating that they may be alert or mildly inquisitive in the current situation (for example, when a track is played or your baby is present). These signs are generally non-threatening and not usually a concern, but your cat should be monitored to ensure they do not develop into signs outlined in behaviour groups B or C.

Watchful or curious – ooh, what's that?

- Alert, interested, curious, moving and leaning forward to investigate
- Head, neck and tail up and tense
- Eyes wide and round
- Ears pricked
- Whiskers held out sideways or forward
- Sniffing the air with a twitching nose

Behaviour group B

Your cat may exhibit *one or more* of these signs, indicating that they may be uncomfortable or anxious in the current situation.

Timid, nervous or anxious

❖ Moving slowly and slinking around
❖ Trying to avoid, escape or hide
❖ Pacing
❖ Body frozen and breath held
❖ Head low and looking away
❖ Forehead furrowed
❖ Mouth tense
❖ Ears sideways or back
❖ Eyelids open wide with pupils dilated
❖ Sniffing the ground
❖ Tail low, tucked between the legs or curled around feet
❖ Suddenly grooming, scratching or licking themselves

Irritated or over-stimulated

- ❖ Body and paws tense
- ❖ Head up
- ❖ Eyes hard and staring with dilated pupils
- ❖ Ears turned back or to the side
- ❖ Tail twitching, waving or flicking
- ❖ Skin and fur rippling or twitching
- ❖ Showing teeth, possibly with a hiss or growl

Behaviour group C

Your cat may exhibit *one or more* of these signs, indicating that they may be very anxious or fearful in the current situation and may become aggressive. These are serious signs, and your cat should be carefully removed from the situation, or from whatever is worrying your cat, immediately. It may be safer to remove whatever is worrying the cat rather than risking injury to yourself by trying to move a potentially aggressive cat.

Frightened, startled

- ❖ Moving away or leaning backwards to avoid the scary thing
- ❖ Cowering with an arched back and fur sticking up
- ❖ Body tense and low to the ground
- ❖ Tail bristled, tense and erect or held low under the body
- ❖ Eyes fully open with a hard stare and dilated pupils — may see whites of their eyes
- ❖ Ears back and flat against the head
- ❖ Whiskers back and flat against the face
- ❖ Yowling, growling, hissing or spitting
- ❖ Panting or rapid breathing
- ❖ May raise a paw as a threat
- ❖ Will escape if possible; if not, may attack

Defensive – 'back off'

❖ Crouched, back arched, leaning away or lying on their back ready to defend
❖ Tail between their legs, wrapped around the body, or erect and bristled
❖ Forehead furrowed and scowling, nose wrinkled, face tense
❖ Eyes wide and staring, pupils dilated
❖ Ears flat back against the head
❖ Whiskers back against the face, mouth open
❖ Meowing loudly, growling, hissing, or spitting
❖ Tail erect and fluffed up

Terrified, ready to attack

❖ Body tense and turned to the side to appear bigger
❖ Back arched or straight with a low head
❖ Fur sticking up
❖ Eyes hard and staring with dilated pupils
❖ Mouth open, baring teeth, jaw tense, lips tight
❖ Whiskers bristling forward
❖ Ears flat against the head
❖ Tail tense and may be up and bristled or low and swishing
❖ Growling, yowling or hissing
❖ Claws out
❖ Trying to intimidate with charges, batting/swiping with their paws and/or snapping
❖ Will fight savagely if there is no other way out

Behaviour group D

These signs are generally non-threatening and not usually of concern *unless* they are directed towards humans, including a baby or doll. If this is the case then these signs are more serious and you need to seek assistance from an appropriate veterinarian immediately.

If these behaviours are only directed at non-human-like objects, then they are not a concern, but your cat should still be monitored to ensure they do not develop into signs outlined in behaviour groups B or C.

Playful, stalking, predatory

❖ Body crouched or stalking, tense, weight forward
❖ Bottom wiggling and rear legs dancing
❖ Head low
❖ Tail low and twitching
❖ Eyes steady and focused, pupils somewhat dilated
❖ Ears forward and erect
❖ Whiskers forward
❖ Grabbing the 'prey', biting it, wrestling it to the floor, or kicking it with their hind feet. (Fine, unless it's you or your baby!)

7
Sounds like a baby!

Why play baby sounds to my cat?

A cat's hearing is much more sensitive than a human's, especially to higher pitched sounds such as a baby crying. Unfamiliar sounds and noises can easily cause excitement, anxiety, agitation, nervousness and fear in any cat. This is especially true if your cat is already reactive to certain noises (for example, thunderstorms or fireworks). These types of responses are common and can make introducing your baby to your cat difficult. Some cats hide under the bed for days when they first hear a baby's cry! Clearly this sort of response has the potential to upset you and the start of life with your new baby.

Playing these tracks now, before the baby arrives, will give you some idea of whether your cat is likely to react unfavourably to baby noises. By playing the tracks and following steps 1 to 5 outlined later in this chapter, you will be able to help your cat become accustomed to the sounds associated with a new baby; this will help to reduce any unfavourable responses.

Playing the tracks*

> ## Observe closely how your cat reacts to the sounds

Introduce the sounds gradually, so as not to worsen your cat's responses to these new noises (see steps 1 to 5). It is also very important to observe your cat closely to see how they are reacting to the sounds. Pay attention to your cat's behaviour and body language while the sounds are playing, and work out which one of the four main behaviour groups (A, B, C or D) they fit into.

After completing steps 1 to 5 and monitoring your cat's responses using the behaviour groups, you will have prepared your cat well for the different sounds that accompany a new baby. You will also be able to identify potential problems and know if you need assistance from an appropriate veterinarian.

If you have two or more cats, it is preferable to work with each cat separately, performing all assessments and training outlined in this book to ascertain each cat's individual reaction. Once you have done this, repeat the assessment with all the cats together. This includes steps 1 to 5 (with the sounds) and the initial introductions when your baby arrives home.

The baby and toy sounds used in both *Tell Your Cat You're Pregnant* and *Tell Your Dog You're Pregnant* have been specifically remastered for animals. They are to be used with care to prepare either cats or dogs, or both, for a new baby. It is critical, when using the sounds, to follow the detailed step-by-step guides and to monitor your pet's behaviour in light of the specific behaviour groups outlined in the relevant book. The same sounds are used for both dogs and cats.

---

*The baby and toy sounds can be downloaded free as MP3 tracks from **http://goo.gl/tYpnZb**

The cat who didn't like YouTube

A couple of years ago, Melissa rang me to discuss a problem she had with her cat, Fergus. Melissa was expecting a baby and her partner, Sam, had read somewhere that it was a good idea to play baby sounds to help prepare a cat for the arrival of a new baby. He went to YouTube and searched for 'baby sounds for cats'. Finding a video he thought was suitable, but which had not been specifically remastered for animals, he loaded it into their sound system and pressed play.

The response from Fergus was instant. From resting comfortably in the sun on the couch, he sprang over the coffee table, smashed a vase and ran straight under the spare bed. Now he was only coming out at night to go to the toilet and have some food, which Melissa left next to the bed. He was clearly petrified by the sudden sounds of a baby and, naturally, Melissa and Sam were quite concerned.

I explained to Melissa that, unfortunately, well-meaning cat owners commonly experienced this situation. Playing downloaded baby sounds to a cat without following a prescribed protocol is a recipe for disaster. Preparing a cat for a baby using recorded sounds needs to be done in a careful, gradual way. It is also advisable to use baby sounds that have been specifically designed for a cat's hearing range. I told Melissa that all was not lost, and this was a problem that we had time to work on.

The first thing was to encourage Fergus to rejoin the family. We achieved this by taking things slowly and encouraging Fergus out from under the bed with his favourite treats as well as regular play with his special toys. We installed a pheromone diffuser in the spare bedroom and also one in the living area. After several weeks and much enticing, Fergus regained his courage to be part of the family routine and once again seemed comfortable in the house.

Melissa and Sam were now concerned about Fergus responding in the same undesirable way when they played baby sounds – or, worse still, responding in the same way when their real baby arrived! I gave them a copy of the baby and toy sounds that have been specifically designed for pets, and the protocol for using these sounds, which are outlined in this book. I advised them not to use sounds from the internet and to ensure that the program was gradual. Melissa thanked me and said she would stay in touch.

Six months later I rang for an update. Their baby, Max, had arrived and Melissa said that he had quite a set of lungs! She thought that the neighbours at the end of the street could hear Max when he got wound up. Immediately my thoughts turned to Fergus – how was he coping? Fergus had adapted perfectly, Melissa said. The training they had implemented, with cat-specific baby sounds and toy noises, meant Fergus had barely responded to Max's first cries at home. This was music to my ears – unlike the screaming from Max I could hear in the background.

Using the sounds and observing

Before playing any of the tracks to your cat, it is important to read the entire book. By all means play the sounds to yourself, but *not* to your cat until you are ready to follow steps 1 to 5 outlined below.

❖ Start with short training sessions (for example, five to ten minutes) and lengthen the sessions gradually; your cat needs time to adjust to the new sounds.

❖ Do not attempt to complete all of the steps in one day or even one week. Take your time over a period of weeks, and advance to the next step only when your cat is relaxed and calm.

❖ Your cat's response may depend on the quality of your speakers, so try to use the best quality stereo system available.

❖ Babies' cries have a high pitch, so ensure the treble is turned to high on your sound system, not the bass.

❖ For step 1 (the observation step), start playing the tracks consecutively at a real-life volume. As soon as you notice a change in your cat's body language associated with playing the sounds (that is, behaviour groups A, B, C or D), then immediately stop playing the sounds and move to step 2.

❖ Steps 2 to 5 explain how to best prepare your cat for the sounds and routines associated with a baby.

❖ For steps 2 and 3, the tracks are initially played at a very low volume that does not cause a fearful response in your cat. The volume is slowly and gradually increased over a period of weeks. Play the tracks while you are doing something very enjoyable and highly distracting with your cat. Essentially, you want the sounds to be associated with good things rather than something scary. During these steps it is very important to monitor the behaviour group signs to ensure your cat is comfortable and relaxed at all times.

❖ In steps 4 and 5 you are setting up household routines that will occur when your baby arrives. These routines create certainty and predictability in both your mind and your cat's mind, which helps to lower everyone's anxiety.

❖ Steps 4 and 5 will also highlight certain situations that may require further assistance from an appropriate veterinarian.

> **The sounds should always be associated with good activities**

The 5 steps

> **Step 1: Play the sounds at a real-life volume once only – observe and assess your cat**

Step 1

This is an observation step. **Only perform this step once,** or you could worsen your cat's response to the sounds.

While the tracks are playing, observe your cat and gauge their reaction. Do not try to interact with your cat or even direct them towards the sounds. Just play the tracks and observe. As soon as your cat responds to the sounds (that is, behaviour groups A, B, C or D) immediately stop playing the tracks and move to step 2. If you continue playing the sounds after you cat is reacting to them it could make their future responses to the sounds worse.

Some cats will not respond to the tracks. They will show none of the signs outlined in behaviour groups A, B, C or D and will act as if they have not even heard the sounds. Assuming that your cat's hearing is normal, then this lack of response can be attributed to one of two reasons:

1. Your cat is not bothered by the sounds of babies; or
2. Your cat does not associate the sounds coming from a stereo system with real baby sounds. In this case your cat may only respond to the noises of a baby when a real baby is present.

If your cat does not respond to the sounds, go to step 4. You will need to monitor your cat's behavioural responses more closely when they hear your actual baby for the first time. If they then continually respond unfavourably (behaviour groups B, C or D) to your actual baby's noises, you will need to seek the assistance of an appropriate veterinarian.

Step 2: Do something your cat enjoys while playing the sounds at a very low volume

Step 2

Your cat is reacting to the sounds. This is common. Now, replay at the *lowest audible volume* all the tracks. Remember, your cat's hearing is extremely sensitive. While the tracks are playing, do something really fun with your cat. You will know what your cat enjoys. For many cats, it is mealtime or food rewards; for other cats, it is playing with their favourite toy, or being groomed or stroked. You want your cat to associate good things with the sounds, and every time a baby sound is heard you want it to be a positive experience. You should be able to distract your cat, so they no longer display the signs outlined in behaviour groups A, B, C or D while the tracks are playing. Play the tracks several times a day at the lowest volume while doing an enjoyable activity.

Continue doing this until your cat appears to be ignoring the sounds or prefers to focus on you or the enjoyable activity and shows none of the signs in behaviour groups A, B, C or D. Now go to step 3.

> **Step 3: Slowly increase the volume of the sounds and repeat step 2 at this new volume**

Step 3

Congratulations! Your cat no longer reacts to any of the tracks being played at the *lowest audible volume*. Next, *slowly* increase the volume of each individual track. For each slight increase in volume, do something fun with your cat while the track is playing. Repeat this until your cat appears to be ignoring the sounds or prefers to focus on you or the enjoyable activity and shows none of the signs in behaviour groups A, B, C or D. Continue to increase the volume gradually, until it is at a volume that you would expect in real life. Obviously the feeding and bath-time tracks need to be quieter.

Play the tracks at different times of the day and night. Remember, babies can scream at around 110 decibels, which is similar to an ambulance siren or a motorcycle, and babies' cries *always* sound louder to tired parents in the middle of the night!

If you are going to use a baby monitor, play the tracks through this as well, to accustom your cat to the noise coming from different areas in the house as well as the different quality of sound.

When your cat no longer displays the signs outlined in behaviour groups A, B, C or D, or can easily be distracted by you when any of the tracks are played at real-life volume levels, go to step 4.

> ## Step 4: Practise where (in real life) you would like your cat to be for tracks 1 to 11

Step 4

Step 4 involves using only tracks 1 to 11 of the baby sounds and toy noises. Each of these tracks is a sound from a specific situation that will occur with your baby every day. For each track, set up the scenario of where you will be, where your baby will be and what your cat will be doing. For instance, baby-feeding time may be on the couch with your baby on your lap. Where will your cat be? Obviously, they cannot be on your lap too. Decide now where you would like your cat to be, and start training them to go to that area at this time. It may be as simple as providing a cat bed for your cat next to the couch and giving a long-lasting tasty treat in this area to encourage them to remain there while you feed. You may need to do this in several rooms, just as some activities will occur in different rooms. Also, play the tracks in a separate room from where you and your cat are, as your baby will not always be in the same room as you.

New parents often move suddenly and appear anxious when their baby starts crying. When you play the track of a baby crying or screaming in another room, it can be useful to get up suddenly and rush towards the sound. At the same time, throw your cat a tasty food treat. These sudden movements and associated food rewards will prepare your cat for your likely movements when your baby starts crying.

Step 4 may require a longer period of time and more effort, depending on your cat's temperament and 'trainability'. This step sets up a clear routine for you and your cat for what you both should be doing at certain times. This consistency helps lower unpredictability and stress in the cat's environment. Once you have each scenario worked out for tracks 1 to 11, continue to step 5.

Step 5: Repeat step 4 using a pretend baby

Step 5

Add a pretend baby to what you did in step 4. This may be a doll or a teddy bear, or even just a large rolled-up towel or a cushion wrapped in a blanket. This may feel like a strange thing to do, but it enables you to practise the same scenarios as in step 4, this time with your hands full.

Place your pretend baby in each of the new items (for example, cot or crib or change table) and perform the activities you are likely to do with your baby while considering where you would like your cat to be at this time.

If you are going to use a baby swing, prepare your cat by placing your pretend baby in the swing and turning it on at the slowest and quietest setting to gauge your cat's response. Even after following these steps you should still supervise or separate your baby and cat when using a swing as your cat could easily be seeking warmth and cuddle up to your baby in the swing.

Currently, all baby talk in the house is probably directed at your cat (or your partner …). This is going to change! Start talking baby talk to the pretend baby, and more adult-style talk to your cat. This will get your cat used to baby language being used for others in the house as well.

When you finish this step, you should be able to play the first eleven tracks at real-life volume, have a 'baby' in your arms, and coo and talk sweet nothings to your 'baby' while your cat is behaving as requested. Your cat is now ready for the sounds of your real baby.

If you get stuck at step 2 or 3, or your cat is consistently displaying concerning behaviour(s) (behaviour group B, C or D), you need the assistance of an appropriate veterinarian.

There may be other everyday sounds that cause your cat to react unfavourably. These might be the doorbell, telephone, or the TV.

Record these sounds and proceed through steps 2 and 3 to decrease your cat's response to the noise.

Whose toy is that?

Cats can be scared of new toy noises

Your baby is not the only new arrival to the house that brings new sounds. Toys will start to appear even before your baby arrives. Some cats can react quite fearfully to unique toy noises. Other cats react markedly only to the sound of squeaky toys. A track of common baby-toy noises (track 12), as well as a track consisting purely of squeaky toys (track 13), are included with this book to accustom your cat to these sounds. Follow through steps 1 to 3 outlined above to habituate your cat to these toy sounds as you replay tracks 12 and 13.

Some baby toys can be dangerous for cats

Some children's toys can be very enticing for cats. Many toys have ribbons, strings or elastic bands on them, which, if swallowed by a cat, can cause an intestinal blockage. Some other smaller items or toys can be a lot of fun for cats to bat around and chase across the floor. Again, if swallowed, these can cause problems. Ideally all of these types of toys and items should be cleaned up after play and kept separate from your cat.

Keep the cat's toy box elevated so your cat does not have continual access to all their toys, and your child is unable to go exploring through the cat-only toy box (see Chapter 10: Preparing your cat).

8

Supervising, separating and training

Supervision

It is critical to supervise your cat and
baby whenever they are together

This book and its associated training methods and techniques do not replace the need for constant adult supervision of your baby and cat. What is constant adult supervision? It means that if your cat and baby are in the same room, or near each other, you should be present, attentive and at all times no more than an arm's length from your baby or your cat, or both. This applies even when one or both of them are asleep.

If you cannot supervise their interactions closely enough, you need to separate your cat and your child until you are again able to monitor them closely. This includes all cats, even those with excellent temperaments. If your cat currently exhibits aggression towards babies, or you are unsure how to interpret your cat's behaviour, seek assistance from an appropriate veterinarian.

Allowing your cat access to the nursery *under supervision* is desirable. This includes after your baby is born. Denying your cat access to the nursery may make them associate the baby with a loss of interaction with you or they may become persistent in trying to get into the nursery to explore the new items. This may mean they try to sneak in when you are not aware. Don't punish or scold them if they jump on or investigate items you would rather they didn't touch, as this might make them fearful or aggressive towards you or the baby. Rather, gently remove them and/or encourage them to return to areas where they are allowed using food rewards or a favourite toy.

Harnesses and leashes

Training a cat to wear a harness with a leash attached is a great way for you to actively supervise your cat during times when you need to have them under control (for example, first introductions with the baby).

Cats who have never worn a harness need to be introduced to it gradually. There are several different types of harnesses available for cats and you may need to experiment to find the one your cat finds most comfortable. Initially the harness should be placed on the cat only at meal times or when getting a tasty food reward and then removed when the treat time is finished. Over time these periods can be extended until your cat is comfortable walking around the house wearing the harness. Then a lightweight leash can be fastened to the harness so the cat can get used to dragging this around. At first they are likely to play with it – after all, it is an in-built chase toy! Do not leave your cat unsupervised wearing a harness and/or leash. When they seem comfortable dragging the leash around, start picking up the leash and 'walking' them indoors. You now have some control over your cat, if needed, and you can also easily reward them with treats for showing calm and relaxed behaviour around the baby.

If you want to start walking your cat outside using the harness and leash, be sure to take it slowly. Many cats are anxious on their first few outings. Start with short sessions and, if your cat seems anxious, move back inside and try again later. Gradually increase the length of these outings and eventually your cat will look forward to their walks.

Two determined girls

Zara and Audrey, two girls aged eight and six, really wanted to take Monty, their four-year-old cat, for walks outside in their garden. Monty was currently not allowed outdoors, but Zara and Audrey had read that walks in the garden would help enrich his life. They wanted to show me what Monty did whenever they put a harness on him – he just flopped down on his side and refused to move. Both Zara and Audrey thought this was hilarious, but these determined girls wanted a solution, so the pressure was on!

I told the girls that Monty needed to get used to wearing the harness. We decided to start by only buckling up the section around his neck while feeding him his favourite dinner. The harness was then to come off when he finished dinner, and hopefully before he noticed it was on. They were to do this for two weeks and then move to buckling the strap around his waist. After this I gave them further detailed written instructions on how to gradually get him used to the harness and leash in a slow, graduated fashion. Having daughters myself, I imagined that Zara and Audrey might become distracted by other endeavours, and that poor Monty would never progress to enjoying the outdoors.

Nearly six months later, Zara and Audrey came in to the cat-only waiting room at the clinic, beaming cheekily. They had done it! Strutting in next to them on a leash and harness was Monty, clearly enjoying the freedom. This is a story I often recount to clients who tell me that their cat refuses to walk on a harness and leash. But do beware: walking a cat on a leash into a veterinary clinic waiting room with other animals and people around could be dangerous, so best bring them in a carrier!

Separation

> Separating your cat and baby
> is critical at certain times

Throughout this book you will read of the need to place your cat in a 'safe and secure area' or to 'separate your cat from your baby'. *Separation is different from supervision.* Separation means that there is a physical barrier between your cat and baby that cannot be breached by either of them. This usually means a room with a closed solid door or internal (framed flywire) screen door, preferably with a lock.

The lock should prevent anyone inadvertently opening the door, such as older children or unsuspecting visitors.

Carriers, crates and cat condos (see below) can also provide separation as long as children cannot reach through the barrier into the cat's space and it also has a solid locking mechanism. This means that your cat and baby are separated until you are available to adequately supervise them again. Barriers, baby gates or playpens that a cat can leap over, and doors that do not properly close, are not adequate for separation.

> Never use the safe, secure areas as punishment

Some cats dislike being confined and have to learn to relax and be comfortable in a separate room, carrier, crate or condo. Train your cat to go into this safe, secure area by throwing tasty food treats into the area and saying 'go to your bed' or similar. Over a period of weeks to months, gradually lengthen the amount of time your cat is confined. Check on them regularly and reward them with something they enjoy (for example, tasty food rewards, play, petting or grooming) for being calm in the area. This will make separation a pleasant experience for your cat and allow you to confidently confine them when necessary, knowing your cat will not become upset. It will also mean you can move your cat into a safe, secure area when you have your hands full with a baby, using voice commands. If cats have been trained to find the crate or carrier a safe haven where good things happen, they can be safely placed inside for short periods (for example, when you are cooking dinner or on the phone). When you are prepared again to supervise your cat and baby then open the door to allow them out. If they do not voluntarily come out of the area, do not force them.

Never use the safe, secure areas as punishment, and regularly check on your cat in this area and ensure they are comfortable.

Carriers

A carrier is usually used to transport your cat to the veterinarian. The ideal carrier opens from the front as well as having an easily removable top half, so that a timid cat can remain in the bottom half of the carrier during the veterinary examination.

An unrestrained cat inside a car could be dangerous for you, your baby and your cat. Solid plastic cat carriers can easily be secured with a seatbelt to keep your cat and family safe during car travel. The carrier should be out of reach of your baby. If your cat has problems with car travel, including motion sickness, you need to seek advice from your veterinarian.

Training a cat to enjoy confinement in a carrier is very helpful for the first introductions with your baby. If you are concerned about how your cat might react during this introduction, you can place your cat in their carrier, assess their body language (using the behaviour groups) and easily reward them for calm, relaxed behaviour, but also easily remove them if they are showing more concerning behaviours (behaviour group B, C or D).

If your cat already associates the carrier with frightening experiences, such as trips to the veterinarian, you will need to proceed slowly. Place the carrier where the cat usually sleeps or relaxes. Remove the door and the top and place your cat's favourite blanket in the bottom and spray the carrier with Feliway (see 'Feliway' in Chapter 9: Staying healthy). When you can entice your cat into the carrier, make the experience enjoyable by praising, petting and playing with your cat or feeding your cat some tasty treats.

When you are confident your cat is relaxed and comfortable in the carrier, reattach the top and allow them to get used to it once more. When your cat accepts both the top and the bottom, then you can add the door.

Once your cat regularly enters the carrier at home and uses it for resting, the carrier door should be closed, and the cat carried in the carrier from one room to another, again giving praise, treats and pets for calm behaviour.

Crates

A crate is a large carrier. It is usually large enough to contain food and water, bedding and also a litter box. Crates are not as portable as carriers.

Condos

A condo is a large, tall crate with several resting levels, and is a permanent fixture in a quiet place in the house. These can be great for smaller living spaces or when there is no dedicated safe haven or room to which the cat can retreat.

Cat-only safe havens

This is an area that *only* your cat can enter and exit. This is different from a 'safe, secure area' where your cat *cannot* enter or exit as they please.

Providing your cat with a separate room or quiet space that allows them to escape household stresses and not be bothered by young children will especially assist anxious or fearful cats when the new baby arrives.

Cats in their safe haven should be left alone

Entry can be restricted to only your cat by:

- ❖ placing a baby gate across the door that only your cat can jump over;
- ❖ placing a door securely propped slightly open so only your cat can squeeze through; or
- ❖ installing a cat flap in the door.

Crates, carriers and condos can also provide a dedicated safe haven as long as the door is left open and mobile children cannot harass or corner your cat.

This safe haven should have fresh food and water, a litter box, scratching posts and hiding places, toys, and places to sit, sleep or rest. For particularly anxious or fearful cats, playing a radio in the room may mask upsetting baby noises, and using Feliway (see 'Feliway' in Chapter 9: Staying healthy) can help create a stress-free area. Remember, when your cat retreats to their safe haven, they should be left in peace.

Sleeping arrangements

If your cat is currently sleeping in the room that the baby is likely to be sleeping in (for example, the nursery or your bedroom) then this needs to change well before the baby arrives, so your cat does not associate the change with the arrival of the baby. From now on, your cat should only be allowed into the nursery when supervised. Supervision means you are *in the nursery with them* when they are exploring the room and you *remove your cat from the room* when you exit.

If you are planning for your baby to sleep in bed with you (consult your paediatrician regarding current SIDS guidelines) or in your bedroom in a cot or crib, or you are planning to give some feeds in bed, your cat should not be sleeping on your bed or even in your bedroom. While you are asleep or just dozing (as mothers often do when feeding), it is not possible to monitor interactions between your cat and your baby. It is not uncommon for a cat to surreptitiously crawl into a warm bed with exhausted parents! This may mean you need to keep the bedroom door shut or install an internal (framed flywire) screen door.

> Make any changes well before your baby arrives

Be aware that unsupervised cats can enter through open windows, so ensure that a flyscreen is fitted on the window to deter your cat or unknown (stray) cats from entering the nursery or bedroom — not to mention flies and insects!

Also be aware that the nursery is not the only place that your baby is likely to fall asleep or be sleeping. Babies will often fall asleep in the stroller, car seat, swing or rocker, portable cot or crib or even on the floor. At all times, ensure you know where your cat is located and if you are not supervising them, separate them to a safe, secure area.

Providing your cat with a cosy, inviting hideaway (see 'Cat-only safe havens' earlier) will help keep them from invading your room or the baby's room and provide alternative sleeping and hiding options to the baby's bed or your bed.

Safely and securely separating your cat from your baby when your baby is unsupervised (in their cot or crib) in the nursery is very important and the most reliable way to do this is to use a physical barrier. A closed solid door, internal (framed flywire) screen door or wooden screen door with a child-proof latch are the safest and simplest options — some cats are very good at pushing open a door without a latch. Ideally this door should also be self-closing.

One tall or two smaller baby gates, stacked on top of each other, could prevent a cat from accessing the nursery. Ensure that your cat can't jump over them or squeeze between the bars. This setup can sometimes be problematic for parents trying to easily access the nursery. Similarly a solid wooden door cut in half (like a stable door) *may* deny your cat access but still enable you to see and hear your baby from outside the room.

Whichever safe, secure door you choose, you should implement this change early in your pregnancy so your cat can get used to being shut out of the nursery at certain times. Allow the cat access to the nursery when you are present so they can investigate all the changes and the new sights, sounds and smells that are happening in the room as items are added.

There are many unsuitable recommendations that are often suggested for deterring your cat from sleeping or jumping into the empty cot or crib *before the baby is born*. These include passive deterrents, active deterrents and some physical barriers. These methods (listed below) do not provide safe, secure separation and are *not* recommended.

1. Passive deterrents placed in the empty cot or crib (before the baby arrives):
   - aluminium foil or double-sided sticky tape on the mattress
   - upside-down plastic carpet protector
   - empty washed aluminium cans
   - containers filled with water
   - loose plastic bags or marbles

> These methods do not provide safe, secure separation and are not recommended

2. Active deterrents (before the baby arrives):
- balloons in the empty cot or crib that will pop when a cat lands on them
- mats that give off static electric pulses
- cat-repellent sprays or scents (for example, citrus)
- spray bottles and water pistols
- motion-activated spray or noise deterrents
- upside-down mouse traps or similar devices
- punishing or yelling at the cat when they jump in the cot or crib
- electric 'shock' collar invisible barrier systems

3. Unsuitable physical barriers
- internal (frameless) screen doors
- cot or crib tent or (mosquito) netting (see text box below)

The problem with the passive and active deterrents listed above, is that they cannot be used when your baby is actually in the cot or crib. So you are relying on your cat remembering past bad experiences when they jumped into the crib to deter them from jumping into the crib again, when the baby is present. This may work for some cats but cannot be guaranteed to work for *all* cats. Once the baby is in the crib, any cat that wants to get into the crib, looking for comfort and warmth, can easily do so without any deterrent. This is far from ideal.

Furthermore, many of these methods employ techniques that can make some cats fearful of the crib or even of their owner, and this does not create the harmonious family environment that we want with a new baby. Ideally, we do not want anything frightening or scary associated with the baby and its surroundings – cats find babies scary enough as it is!

Internal frameless screen doors are flimsy and can easily be breached by a cat pushing through them. For this reason they are not recommended.

Tents and netting

A word of caution about cot or crib tents and (mosquito) netting. In the past, a particular brand of cot or crib and play-yard tent was recalled by the relevant safety authorities due to 'infants and toddlers being at risk of serious injury or death due to strangulation and entrapment hazards presented by these products', and 'one fatality and one serious injury that occurred between January 1997 and April 2012'. While this may not be the case for all brands of cot or crib tents currently and previously on the market, it is important to assess the relevant safety standards and hazards on any such device before fitting it to your baby's cot. Keep in mind that this is a higher rate of death and injury than the rate for cats smothering babies (see Chapter 2: Common myths and problems).

That's my chair!

John and Jenny were tired, not because of their new baby, Miranda, but because of their cat, Tuppy, disturbing the peace. Tuppy would not settle in the evening and was meowing and pacing up and down the hallway, often scratching at the closed nursery door. The noise was keeping them awake at night, and John and Jenny had tried everything to keep him quiet. Thankfully, the noise didn't seem to bother Miranda.

Apart from the evenings, Tuppy was behaving normally. He didn't seem particularly bothered by Miranda's presence and even lay next to the baby when she had playtime on her mat. It seemed odd that the new behaviour was only occurring at night and John wondered if Tuppy was jealous of Miranda. Was this his way of getting revenge?

After chatting with John and Jenny, the cause for Tuppy's angst became obvious. Miranda's room had previously been Tuppy's favourite place to sleep, especially on the cosy chair that was now Jenny's feeding chair. After Miranda arrived, his owners were concerned about stories of cats smothering babies and locked him out of this area. A couple of times he managed to sneak into the room, and his owners found him snoozing on his favourite chair, uninterested in the baby sleeping nearby.

Clearly, Tuppy was upset with the sudden change to his environment and routine and was having trouble adjusting. I reassured John and Jenny that Tuppy was not jealous of Miranda, but rather just wanted his favourite place to sleep back.

We decided to move the favourite chair to a position just outside the nursery door. The plan was to then move it gradually to a more suitable location over the next few weeks. A new nursing chair would be purchased for Jenny.

Tuppy would be allowed access to the nursery when John and Jenny were present. We created two elevated perches for Tuppy to rest on while his owners were using the nursing chair or change table. They were to reward him with tasty treats for relaxing in these areas.

The wooden nursery door was replaced with a flywire screen door so Tuppy could look into the room when he was not allowed in. This helped him to settle. When they started gradually moving his favourite chair, often his owners would find him resting on the carpet just outside the door while Miranda was sleeping. They even placed a cat bed there for him to relax on.

John rang me two weeks later to thank me for the best night's sleep he'd had in months. Tuppy was much more relaxed in the evenings and now really enjoyed the interactions in the nursery throughout the day. John was relieved that the sleepless nights with Tuppy were over.

Training your cat

The old saying that 'dogs have masters and cats have slaves' may be humorous but is not entirely correct. Many owners believe that it is not possible to train cats, but cats can be trained in the same way as dogs: by using rewards. The only difference is that cats are usually slower to eat any food rewards offered, and this should be allowed for before requesting the next behaviour.

Cats can be trained using food rewards

Training your cat enables you to have some control over them and also provides them with exercise and fun. Limit the training sessions to only a couple of minutes daily to keep your cat interested.

Currently, you may be using loud noises or claps, water sprays, booby traps or other deterrents or punishment to reprimand or try to control your cat. These methods are not suitable within a family, as you want your cat to associate only good things with your baby. Also, babies and children are physically and mentally unable to interact successfully with a cat in this way. Furthermore, these methods do not create a harmonious home environment in which a child–cat relationship can develop.

The training methods you use should be effective for the entire family and should be based on rewarding desirable behaviours and ignoring or redirecting unfavourable behaviours. To make sure the relationship between your cat and baby is a happy one, good things need to occur whenever your baby is around.

Make good things happen for your cat when your baby is present

When training your cat you need to find a reward that they value highly. For most cats this will be a very tasty treat, but for other cats it may be petting or play with a favourite toy. Whichever it is, give that reward when your cat performs the behaviour you want them to learn. Common treats that cats love are:

- cooked chicken
- small shrimps or prawns
- dried liver or bacon
- small pieces of cheese or cream cheese flavoured with salmon (but be aware that some cats are lactose intolerant)
- plain yoghurt
- tuna or tuna oil or paste
- wet cat food
- Nuttelex® or butter
- smooth peanut butter
- yeast spreads (for example, Marmite® or Vegemite®)
- anchovy paste
- commercial cat treats

Place several containers filled with small treats around the house out of your cat's reach. They should be only accessible to adults. This will enable you to instantly reward your cat for appropriate behaviour without missing an opportunity.

There are many different behaviours that your cat can be trained to perform, but the most important ones for a cat belonging to a pregnant owner are:

- teaching your cat to get 'down' or 'off' an area (for example, the kitchen bench) (see instructions below)
- training your cat to wear a harness and leash (see earlier in this chapter)
- training your cat to 'go to bed' in their safe, secure area (see earlier in this chapter)

Teaching your cat 'down'

This requires very simple training and involves throwing a tasty food reward away from you and onto the floor for your cat while pointing towards it and saying 'down' or similar. Try to be consistent, using the same word and hand signal each time. Over time and with repetition your cat will start to associate your pointing finger and 'down' word with a treat being present and they will seek the treat, which removes them from the area in which you didn't want them to be.

9

Staying healthy

To keep everyone healthy, first make sure your baby, your cat and your house are kept clean. Second, attend to any health issues immediately. Keep in mind that it is much more likely that your child will catch an infection from another child than from your cat. The advice in this book is only general and if you are considering having a baby, currently pregnant or have young children and are concerned about the health risks of your cat, discuss this with your doctor.

Family hygiene

- Ensure that all family members wash their hands before mealtimes, after playing outside or touching the cat.
- All nappy or diaper buckets should have a firm, sealable lid to prevent their use as a cat drinking bowl. Ensure they will not accidentally open, even when filled with water, tipped on their side and rolled around.
- Soiled disposable nappies or diapers should be placed in bins out of reach of your cat.
- Do not allow your cat to lick your baby's or child's face. This can be dangerous, not only from a behavioural perspective but also because some worms and cat scratch disease (see below) can be spread in this manner. If your cat does lick your baby's face or licks other areas of your baby (for example, the feet), wash the area with soap and water.

❖ Owners are often concerned about the amount of cat fur around their house and the possibility of their baby becoming ill from swallowing fur. Do not be concerned; there is no known link between cat fur and any diseases or allergy-inducing issues.

> A small amount of cat fur
> will not harm a baby

❖ If your baby is unwell or you are concerned about their health, contact your doctor.

Cat bites

While owning a cat can be a delightful family experience and has enormous benefits for the child and the family, parents need to be aware of the risk of injury through cat scratches or bites.

Cat bites are more difficult to treat than dog bites. Cats have long, slender front teeth and almost always inflict puncture wounds that can be difficult to clean and disinfect. Inadequate or delayed treatment can increase the chance of infection and can lengthen recovery time.

> All cat bites should be promptly treated

Here are some facts about cat bites in humans:

❖ About half of all cat bites involve the hand, which indicates most injuries occur when someone tries to touch, pet or pick up the cat.

- Up to eighty per cent of cat bites seen by a doctor become infected and thirty to forty per cent of these require hospitalisation.
- Most studies show that the cat is known to the victim.
- Of all cat bites, around eighty per cent occur in the home or yard.
- Approximately one-third of bites occur when performing innocuous activities such as petting, playing with or feeding the cat.
- Fifteen per cent of cat bites occur when the person tries to break up a cat fight.

Allergies and asthma

Owning a cat may help prevent babies from developing asthma and allergies

Cats are commonly said to be responsible for more asthma and allergic disease than other pets. However, there is currently no evidence to support this notion. Exposure of a baby or child to cats does not increase their chances of developing an allergy; in fact, according to recent studies, living with a cat during your childhood, especially during the first year, could protect against developing allergies. This is related to the current hygiene theory of allergy development, which states that our home environment is too clean (without pets) and this contributes to children developing allergies.

Current research suggests you need *not* be concerned about your children developing asthma or an allergy when deciding whether to keep a cat in the family. Furthermore, if your child develops allergies (to cats) at any stage when growing up, current research states that these will not have been caused by living with a cat. Check with a specialist allergy doctor if you need further information.

Debating the mother-in-law

Lorraine and her toddler, Amber, came to see me with their cat, Sparky. Sparky was scheduled for her regular vaccination but Lorraine also had an unusual question for me.

Lorraine had had several allergies and asthma as a child. Now Amber had developed similar problems. When Amber started getting eczema, Lorraine's well-meaning mother-in-law suggested that Sparky was responsible and that, for Amber's sake, Sparky needed to find a new home.

Lorraine was quite concerned about this: she had owned cats all her life and never considered them to be the source of her allergies and asthma. Lorraine did some research on the internet and found many anecdotal reports of a child's allergies 'disappearing' when there was no longer a cat in the house. This made her believe that rehoming Sparky might solve Amber's allergic responses. Could her mother-in-law be right?

Armed with the latest research, I was able to calm Lorraine's fears. I pointed her to several studies that showed that, for a new baby, owning a cat actually had a protective effect against developing allergies. That is, a child was less likely to develop allergies if they lived with a cat from a young age. I explained to her that a cat made the environment less hygienic, and therefore better for a growing child's immunity.

Lorraine left the clinic that day sporting a huge smile and armed with some relevant information for her mother-in-law. I wished her luck for that conversation!

Keeping your cat healthy

Basic preventative health

❖ Ensure your cat is regularly examined by your veterinarian and is up to date with their vaccinations. Most veterinarians recommend a health check every six to twelve months.

❖ Treat your cat regularly for internal parasites (for example, intestinal worms) and external parasites (for example, fleas, ticks and mites), as some are transmissible to humans. Consult your veterinarian for the products most suitable for your cat and your geographical location. Buy an adequate supply in advance when you are expecting a baby.

> Most veterinarians recommend a health check every six months

❖ Place the cat litter box in an area that your baby cannot reach once they become more mobile. Clean the box regularly. Babies have less resistance than adults to certain causes of gastroenteritis and other diseases caught from faeces.

❖ Trim your cat's claws regularly to avoid accidental scratching. If your cat is not used to having this done, it is a good idea to start well before your baby arrives, so your cat is accustomed to it before the family grows. For advice on trimming your cat's nails contact your veterinarian. If you still find trimming your cat's nails a problem, then acrylic nail caps are available (for example, Soft Claws® or Soft Paws®). These cover the nails with a soft material to prevent injury. They need to be reapplied every four to six weeks, as they fall off with nail growth.

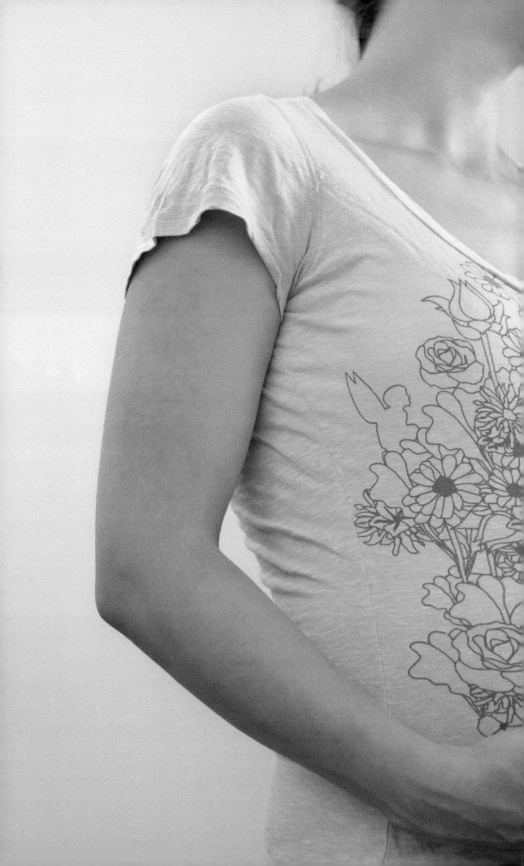

- ❖ If your cat has long fur, ensure it is regularly brushed to avoid knots and tangles. If you cannot brush your cat or they cannot adequately groom themselves, have them professionally groomed regularly.
- ❖ Cat bedding should be washed regularly and carpets vacuumed.
- ❖ Have your cat desexed to decrease the likelihood of wandering, urine spraying and health problems to do with the reproductive system. There is some evidence that desexed male cats are less reactive or aggressive.
- ❖ If your cat develops any skin conditions or gastrointestinal problems, have them examined immediately by a veterinarian, as some of these are contagious for humans. Similarly, if there are skin conditions or gastrointestinal conditions among family members, have your cat examined.
- ❖ Any medical conditions can cause a cat pain or irritation, which may cause them to be less tolerant of changes in their environment and being petted or cuddled. This may lead to toileting issues or aggression. These symptoms are more common in older cats but can occur in younger cats too. Specific problems are arthritis, lameness, teeth problems, thyroid problems, ear infections and skin conditions. It is advisable for your cat to have a complete veterinary examination soon after your pregnancy is confirmed so that any potential problems can be rectified early. Regular blood tests and faecal examinations may also be recommended by your veterinarian.
- ❖ Any changes in your cat's behaviour or routine, or loss of appetite might indicate an underlying medical condition. If your cat's behaviour changes during preparation for your baby's arrival or after the baby comes, see your veterinarian.

This baby is making me itchy!

Furphy, a three-year-old Abyssinian cat, had a problem. He was losing fur and continually licking himself. His owners were finding clumps of fur scattered around the house. They were concerned that he was stressed by the huge change that had occurred when their new baby, Lucy, had arrived six months ago. Everything had gone well with the initial introductions but now he appeared to be over-grooming. His owners believed that this was caused by stress.

Further discussions about Furphy's behaviour revealed that he had adapted quite well to the baby's arrival. He had not had any other behaviour changes and seemed quite calm; he even interacted by rubbing his body and head against Lucy at times. His owners felt that the relationship between Furphy and Lucy was going really well, so the sudden fur loss and excessive licking puzzled them.

After a while, Furphy jumped onto my lap and this gave me a good chance to look at his coat. He had two large bald patches, one near his tail and the other on his belly. Parting his fur, the problem quickly became evident – Furphy had a severe flea infestation! His owners were initially shocked and incredulous but I showed them the little critters crawling through his sparse fur.

Then the light bulb moment came when they both looked at each other – with the busyness of life with a new baby they had forgotten to give Furphy his regular flea treatment. Both owners felt a little sheepish to have missed such a simple thing but also relieved that Furphy was not put out by the presence of Lucy.

Cat scratch disease

Cat scratch disease (CSD) or cat scratch fever is caused by the bacterium *Bartonella henselae*. It is spread to humans by a bite, scratch or lick (on an open wound) from an infected cat or indirectly via cat fleabites – the cat flea can bite both cats and humans.

In healthy people, CSD is usually a self-limiting infection and can cause swollen lymph nodes if severe, as well as malaise, fever, sore throat, headache and backache. Symptoms usually spontaneously resolve in a few months. While this disease is unpleasant, it is not a reason to get rid of your cat.

A recent report on pregnant woman who had contracted CSD during pregnancy did not identify any problems, on follow-up, with their newborn babies.

Fleas and possibly ticks spread the disease between cats. About a third of all cats already have *Bartonella* and infected cats do not display signs of illness.

Avoid rough play or any activities that encourage your cat (or especially a kitten) to scratch or bite, and do not allow cats to lick open wounds such as scratches. Always thoroughly wash cat bites and scratches with soap and running water. Treat your cat for fleas to reduce the chance of them catching the disease.

Medical attention should be sought if your cat causes any injuries to your baby, or yourself. If you are concerned about CSD then discuss this with your doctor.

Ringworm

Ringworm is a skin condition that both cats and humans can catch and, despite its name, is not caused by a 'worm' but rather fungi called dermatophytes. In humans it is called tinea. It is more commonly seen in kittens and children.

In humans, it appears as a red scaly area, and may look like a target with a patch of hair loss. In cats, it causes circular patches of fur loss, commonly on the head and paws.

Ringworm can be transmitted from an infected cat or kitten to humans via direct contact or by contact with such things as infected bedding, furniture or carpet. It can also spread between humans (especially children) via sharing hats, combs, brushes, towels, clothing or sports equipment. Washing hands after handling pets and avoiding direct contact with infected cats helps prevent the spread of ringworm.

If you or your cat develop skin lesions then consult your doctor and/or veterinarian. There are several treatment options available.

Feliway®

Feliway is a synthetic feline pheromone, a copy of a substance that is naturally produced by special glands on your cat's face. It creates familiarity and makes your cat feel safe and secure, regardless of their age or sex, when facing potentially stressful situations, such as meeting a new baby. Your cat applies the pheromone naturally when 'bunting' or rubbing their face on items that they want to make familiar. By copying the cat's natural facial pheromones, Feliway creates a state of familiarity with these items.

It comes in two forms – a plug-in diffuser and a spray. The plug-in diffuser covers 50 to 70 square metres (540 to 750 square feet) and should be placed in the main room in the house, where your cat spends most of their time, at least two weeks before your due date. Replenish with a refill every four weeks. In addition, or alternatively, spray prominent cat-height areas (for example, door frames and cupboard corners) around the house as well as spraying any new furniture (for example, the cot or crib and highchair) or items and objects such as strollers and play mats that you bring into the home. The spray form can also be used to assist with introductions when you first bring the baby home (see Chapter 12: Your baby is born!). It is not recommended to spray it directly onto skin. For more information or to purchase Feliway products go to **www.babyandpet.com.au**.

Medications

- ❖ All cat medications should be stored in a child-proof cabinet.
- ❖ All human medications should be kept well away from your cat (and your baby!), as some can be toxic to cats.
- ❖ Some cats may benefit from anti-anxiety medication to assist with the initial stress of the appearance of a newborn. Many of these medications do not show results instantly and need several weeks to achieve the desired effect, so plan this in advance of your baby's arrival. These medications are only available on prescription from your veterinarian.

10
Preparing your cat

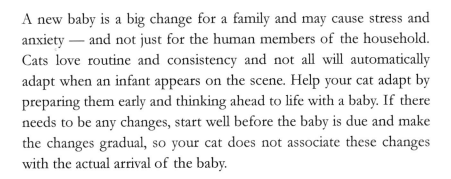

A new baby is a big change for a family and may cause stress and anxiety — and not just for the human members of the household. Cats love routine and consistency and not all will automatically adapt when an infant appears on the scene. Help your cat adapt by preparing them early and thinking ahead to life with a baby. If there needs to be any changes, start well before the baby is due and make the changes gradual, so your cat does not associate these changes with the actual arrival of the baby.

> Make any changes well before
> your baby arrives

If the current location of your cat's resting, sleeping, feeding and playing areas is going to be unsuitable when the baby arrives, you will need to start gradually changing these locations now. Also, if the litter box is currently located in the nursery or an undesirable place once the baby is born, start slowly moving the box, a few inches a day, to the more desirable location. The litter box should be in a private position away from your cat's food and water, and away from busy traffic areas or noisy household appliances, like the washing machine or dryer. Moving the box too quickly can cause your cat to keep toileting in the original spot. If this continues you may need to seek the advice of an appropriate veterinarian.

Changing routines

Certainty and predictability help to minimise anxiety. Cats are creatures of habit and need to feel in control of their environment. They require predictable routines, surroundings and relationships to help them feel comfortable. The chaos of a baby could easily upset this, causing anxiety in your cat. If you plan any changes, these need to be made early on to decrease your cat's anxiety and confusion at a later date.

Many expectant parents feel guilty that they will have less time with their cat when their baby arrives, so they try to increase the playtime and the amount of attention they give their cat before the baby is born. They hope this will be stored in an 'attention bank' that the cat can draw from once the baby arrives. Unfortunately, this can have the opposite effect; in addition to the new little person disrupting the household, the cat becomes more unsettled as the amount of attention they receive goes from unusually high to minimal overnight.

Before your baby is born, introduce a regular schedule that you will realistically be able to adhere to when your baby arrives. Start with play, petting, grooming and feeding schedules. But do not be fooled! A new baby requires an extraordinary amount of time. When you think about feeding a newborn up to eight times a day — and remember that this can take an hour each time — you begin to understand how your time disappears, especially when each feed results in a nappy or diaper change. As well as tending to your new baby, you will be faced with a plethora of chores that need to be performed, not to mention allowing time to just hold, gaze at, cuddle and enjoy your new baby! There will also be extra visitors to see you and your new baby, and they take up further time. All this will be radically different from your current routine. It is unlikely that you will have time to cuddle and sleep with your cat for an hour, or play for long periods when your baby requires three-hourly (or more frequent) feeds and several sleeps during the day.

> ## Schedule regular dedicated time to interact and play with your cat

Gradually decrease the interaction time with your cat over several months to a level that you honestly believe you will be able to manage when your baby arrives. To keep the bond with your cat strong, dedicate a minimum period (for example, ten minutes) twice daily to focusing exclusively on your cat. Once your baby has arrived, the most appropriate time for this may be when another person is available to care for the baby, allowing you to give your cat your full attention. During this time, cuddle, pet, groom and play with your cat with their toys. Try hard to maintain this schedule and make it one that can be easily done when your baby arrives home. Ideally, set a (quiet) alarm or reminder so as not to miss your cat's special time.

Consider whether your cat will be allowed onto the furniture, your bed or onto your lap when the baby arrives. A large cat sitting on your lap may be fine as long as you are not nursing the baby! Retraining your cat so that they will only jump onto your lap when invited is often a compromise. Get your cat used to sitting next to you on the couch so they are not always on your lap.

To train your cat to wait until they are invited to sit on your lap, simply stand up and drop the cat off your lap whenever they jump up uninvited. Next, teach your cat to jump up on your command, using a treat to begin with to encourage them. This will teach them that they only get to sit on your lap when invited, and won't create confusion when you are nursing the baby.

The TV-loving cat

Trisha emailed me for some advice about her cat, Leo. He was being disruptive whenever Trisha sat down on the couch to nurse her newborn baby, Heath. As soon as Trisha would sit down, Leo would jump onto the couch and try to get onto her lap. He would push into Heath with his head and body, trying to make more room on Trisha's lap. This would upset Heath, and he would become reluctant to feed, while Leo continued to secure a comfortable position on Trisha's lap. Heath was becoming so upset that, in exasperation, Trisha had begun locking Leo out of the living room so they could nurse properly. Naturally, Leo wasn't happy with this and had started meowing and scratching at the door to be let back in. Now he had even started spraying urine in some areas around the house. Clearly Leo was not a happy cat!

As we discussed Leo's daily routine and home environment, Trisha mentioned that she had gone on maternity leave two months earlier than planned for medical reasons. During this period, Trisha and Leo had really bonded. They had become accustomed to watching daytime TV, sitting on the couch, with Leo snuggled happily on Trisha's lap. Once Heath had arrived, the daytime ritual of TV soap operas had stopped, and of an evening Trisha was tired and would go to bed rather than sit on the couch and cuddle Leo.

I could see the issue for Leo – all he wanted was a return to the routine of daytime cuddles on the couch. Whenever Trisha sat down, he assumed this is what would happen. Then, when Trisha put him in a separate room, he was even more confused and voiced his frustration. The anxiety associated with a sudden change in routine had also caused poor Leo to start spraying urine.

I suggested that Trisha place a cat bed for Leo next to her on the couch. Initially, she was to train Leo to stay on this bed, using small tasty food rewards and pets whenever she sat on the couch without Heath. She was to do this several times a day for short periods. Eventually, when she sat down with Heath, she was to continue to encourage Leo to relax next to her with food rewards and pets. After a while Leo would learn that, if he relaxed next to her on the couch while she was nursing, good things would happen.

Trisha was also to schedule a ten-minute session twice a day when Leo was allowed on her lap for a good cuddle. During these sessions, she was to place a blanket on her lap so Leo knew that this was his lap time. Ideally, this time was to coincide with Trisha's partner being home, so he could attend to the baby and Leo's special time would not be interrupted.

One month later, Trisha emailed me to tell me that Leo had responded very well to the adjustment in his couch and cuddle routine and relished the twice-daily one-on-one time with her. His urine spraying had stopped as quickly as it had started and it was clear he was much happier with the new routine.

The 'one person' cat

If your cat is especially close to one particular family member, encourage other family members to spend more time with them to hopefully increase your cat's attachment to them. This is especially the case if the most attached person is likely to soon be the most time poor! A good way to start is by having your partner or family member take over fun interactions like feeding, grooming and playtime. If these were always shared activities, the change will make little difference to the cat. If not, the cat will need time to adjust to the new routine as well as the style and skills of the new caregiver.

Din dins time!

Currently you may be feeding elaborate home-cooked meals to your cat. Your new routine is unlikely to be able to accommodate this. Discuss with your veterinarian a suitable, more convenient food. Some cats can be quite fussy and turn their nose up at a sudden change of food. To assist with this change, place the new food in the old bowl and the original food in a novel or different bowl. Start with a small amount of the new food and a normal serve of the original food. Over a period of a couple of weeks, decrease the amount of original food placed out while increasing the amount of the new food. Eventually your cat will be eating mainly the new food, and the original food and novel bowl can be taken away.

Gradually decrease the rigidity of the actual feeding time so your cat does not always expect the food at exactly the same time each day. If your cat does not cope well with this change and becomes demanding around feeding time, buy an automatic feeder to maintain regular, predictable feeding times that do not involve your cat pestering you. Some cats prefer to eat many small meals daily, and purchasing a dry-food dispenser can assist time-poor owners as well as catering to your cat's preference. Food and water bowls should be located where your baby or toddler cannot reach them.

The furry alarm clock

Nina and Stephen didn't need an alarm clock because they owned a cat. Charlie woke them up every morning at 5.45 am. He meowed incessantly, jumped on the bed, purred and rubbed up against his owners until one of them got up and fed him. If Nina and Stephen didn't respond quickly enough to Charlie's begging, he would jump on their heads and occasionally scratch or bite one of them. They tried to keep him out of their bedroom by shutting the door, but Charlie was persistent– he could meow and scratch at the door for hours!

Nina and Stephen were understandably concerned, as they were expecting a baby. They were worried Charlie's behaviour was going to be disruptive and perhaps dangerous for the baby.

When I went to visit Nina, Stephen and Charlie, I found their furry alarm clock to be a very friendly and engaging cat. I discussed at length the various strategies they might consider to reset Charlie's body clock to a more civilised time.

Nina and Stephen needed to establish a feeding source that Charlie did not link to them. This was best provided in the form of an automatic feeder with a timer, which would cater to Charlie at 5.45 am. It would be located far away from the bedroom in the laundry, which adjoins the lounge room. He could easily and comfortably be confined to this area of the house. I prescribed some short-term medication that would help Charlie to sleep during the night and assist him with the change to his routine. I asked Nina and Stephen to also start some vigorous playtimes close to bedtime to tire Charlie out.

I had an update from Stephen two months after my house call. Stephen was very happy to report that Charlie was doing well in his wing of the house during the night. I gave them my best wishes that their new baby would also sleep through the night.

Environmental enrichment

Environmental enrichment (EE) involves making simple changes to your cat's lifestyle and environment to ensure your cat is getting enough physical and mental stimulation. This can assist when owners have less time for their cat once the baby arrives. EE can also help a cat handle a period of change that might otherwise cause anxiety and stress, such as the changes surrounding the arrival of a new baby.

> Environmental enrichment can help a cat cope with a new baby

EE can take several forms: you can change the way you feed your cat, provide more or different social stimulation, add structures to your cat's environment, provide toys and playtime, and increase sensory stimulation. EE encourages a more normal range of behaviours in your cat and serves to constructively occupy their time.

The following strategies are suggestions only. Each cat is an individual, and should be treated as such, with EE strategies tailored to their particular emotional, physical, behavioural and medical needs. For example, an anxious cat needs greater security and may not benefit from a new outdoor enclosure where unknown neighbourhood cats are now visible. Similarly, an arthritic cat that experiences pain jumping or landing will not benefit from a network of cat trees, high shelves and walkways. Ground-level indoor hiding places and the use of gently sloping ramps to lower vantage points may better suit both cats' needs.

Elevated resting places and hidey-holes

When cats are faced with something stressful that may represent a potential threat, they like to hide, preferably in a high, dark, secluded place from which there is a good view, so that the situation can be

assessed in safety. Being able to hide will help your cat cope with the challenges, changes and stress in their environment when a new baby is present. Hiding places can be boxes, crates, baskets, wardrobes or cupboards with the door left open — even carriers provide nice hiding places for cats.

Cats like to hide in high places
with a good view

Cats love to view their surroundings from a high vantage point. This is not because they want to be dominant, but because it allows them to survey the environment from a safe distance for potential threats. For some cats this spot may be on a shelf or on top of a cupboard; for others, it may be the top of the couch or bed. Providing several

elevated resting areas or vantage points for your cat around the house enables them to get away from noise and observe their surroundings. Placing hidey-holes in these elevated areas may also be beneficial for your cat. These can be as simple as an upside-down cardboard box with one side cut out of it for an opening.

Cats spend a lot of time resting and sleeping, so there should be plenty of comfortable areas for them throughout the home. Since they like to move around to sleep where it is warmest, a variety of beds in sunny locations can be useful.

Play and toys

Establish a play schedule for your cat that you can maintain when your baby arrives (see 'Changing routines' earlier).

Toys that move are usually the most successful with cats – the movement triggers a cat's instincts to hunt, chase and pounce – but take notice of the types of toys your cat favours. Cats need an assortment of toys they can chase, bat, roll, pounce on, capture, sink their teeth into and carry. All cats have individual preferences for play, and even older, apparently sedentary cats can enjoy periods of play. Some cats do not like to play at all and need other forms of enrichment and stimulation.

There are many varieties of cat toys available. Some require human interaction while others encourage independent play when owners are busy or absent. Toys that are not obviously connected to the owner's body are a good way to encourage play and discourage biting and scratching of owners' hands or feet. If you have played games in the past that encourage your cat to stalk and attack you or parts of your body, now is the time to replace them with safer games before your baby comes home (see Chapter 4: Aggression).

> Cats usually prefer toys that make sudden movements

172

Cats get used to toys quickly and may tire of them, even after only a few minutes of play, so rotate them regularly to keep your cat interested. Placing catnip or traces of food on the toys may increase your cat's interest.

Check toys regularly for damage, as some cats destroy or eat toys. Whenever you introduce a new toy, always supervise your cat. Loose string, ribbons and wool are not safe for cats to use for play. Keep the cat toy box shut so your cat does not have continual access to all the toys, and prevent your child from picking up and chewing on the cat's toys. See **www.babyandpet.com.au** for recommended cat toys.

Laser pointers

Using laser pointers, torches or reflections from watches or rings to entertain cats is a controversial topic. Some cats become obsessed and frustrated by the light. If you think about it, in their mind it is an object that appears from nowhere, darts around and can *never* be caught. For a cat, not being able to complete the entire stalk, chase, pounce and catch sequence of predatory play behaviour is highly frustrating. There is never any satisfaction in capturing the highly desirable object. These types of cats will often incessantly search for the pointer long after play has finished; they may become anxious and distressed and heavily fixated on it. Some cats can become obsessive and start to chase shadows and other reflections incessantly. If this is your cat, then it's best to use other types of toys (for example, a toy on a string) where your cat has an opportunity to 'catch' the item sometimes. An anxious or frustrated cat is not a good thing to have around a new baby.

Food and treats

Cats in the wild have to find their prey using their sense of smell as well as their vision. Hunting may take a large part of their day, and a cat may eat ten to twenty small meals each day. By making all food available in the bowl, 'foraging time' for an indoor cat has been reduced to a few minutes per day, as compared with the hours needed for natural foraging. Therefore, some environmental enrichment activities should include foraging or problem-solving to get their food.

Placing toys around the house that contain some of the cat's regular meal or special treats can be a great way to encourage your cat to forage and 'hunt' for their food. You can also make mealtime interesting by hiding food, using puzzle feeders, placing food in novel places or where the cat has to jump or climb. Hide treats or toys in different rooms, scatter dry food across the floor or hide it in little nooks and crannies so your cat has to hunt to find its meal. Placing food or treats inside paper, discarded paper-towel rolls, cardboard boxes or old rags allows your cat to tear them apart to get to the food inside. Give your cat something to chew, such as moistened rawhide chews, dried fish, and beef or chicken jerky.

Interactive toys (for example, Kongs®) and puzzle feeders that hold various food items (or the cat's meal) and treats can provide enrichment for your cat. Some cats need to be initially shown how to access the food and treats. Some recommended puzzle feeders and interactive toys can be found at **www.babyandpet.com.au.**

Scratching posts

Provide several scratching posts for your cat. These keep your cat's claws healthy and allow your cat to mark their territory with pheromones and visual signals. Encourage your cat to use the post by placing them onto the post when scratching other areas and then rewarding them with treats and praise. Putting catnip, treats and toys on or near the post can encourage them further. Scratching posts should be sturdy, and made of materials your cat prefers. Locate the scratching post next to a window, or a sleeping or resting area, as cats will often scratch when they stretch after a nap.

Cat trees or scratching posts with platforms or climbing structures, preferably with natural bark or sisal rope, are also good.

Visual enrichment

Cats are inquisitive creatures, so a window with a view of the world, people, animals and birds, will enrich your cat's life. Or you might provide interesting outlooks from vantage points at windows onto busy scenes or activity in the garden (for example, a bird feeder).

Some cats respond to images and sounds on the television, and there are DVDs available that can provide these cats with stimulation (see **www.babyandpet.com.au** for further details). Often the best videos are those showing live action of birds, fish, small mammals and insects. Computer screens savers can entertain some cats, and other cats like to 'play' on iPads or similar touch screens, although these may ultimately be as frustrating as laser pointers (see Laser pointers text box earlier), because the cat is never able to 'catch' the electronic mouse, fish or other prey.

Access to outdoors

An outdoor cat enclosure or run, or walking your cat on a harness and leash, can enrich your cat by providing them with access to the sights, smells and sounds of the garden. Walking a cat on a harness and leash may sound odd to some owners but many cats enjoy walks in the fresh air, which can give them some much-needed stimulation (see Chapter 8: Supervising, separating and training).

Some cats enjoy walks outdoors
on a harness and leash

Options for cat enclosures and runs include:

- modular structures that can be attached to the home;
- freestanding enclosures; or
- cat netting to cover an area such as a balcony, courtyard or part of the backyard.

Cats who have been indoor-only cats but are now going outdoors may require further vaccinations or parasite prevention treatment. This should be discussed with your veterinarian.

Cat plants

Many cats enjoying grazing on non-toxic plants such as cat grass, catmint and catnip. These can be grown inside in a sunny position. These are great for cats to smell and eat, and provide them with sensory enrichment. (Note: about one-third of all cats are indifferent to catnip.) If your cat ignores the plants you've planted, you could try rubbing the plants with a little tuna oil to start off the investigation. If you are unsure if a plant is cat-friendly then check with your veterinarian.

Petting, grooming and interacting with you

Some cats really enjoy one-on-one petting or grooming time with their owner. If this is your cat, try to set up a realistic schedule to allow your cat some of this regularly. It should be reasonably consistent, so try to do it when someone else is home to share the duties.

11
Are you ready?

Preparing the nursery

Familiarising your cat

Cats can become anxious or stressed by change and renovations but, if you introduce your cat to all the new baby items well before the baby arrives, you will minimise the anxiety your cat may feel about this major change in their life. When setting up the nursery, supervise your cat while allowing them to explore the space, the toys, furniture, clothing, stroller, car seat, new smells (baby creams, lotions, etc.) to become familiar with them. Allow your cat to smell and investigate and even rub and 'bunt' them. Do not be concerned about them putting fur or dirt on these things. Reward your cat for correct behaviour with food rewards, praise and pets. Use some of the baby lotions and creams on yourself before the baby is born to allow your cat to get used to new baby smells in a calm, stress-free environment.

To make new objects smell more familiar, spray them with Feliway when they first arrive. You may wish to install a Feliway diffuser to help your cat feel more secure during this potentially stressful time (see Chapter 9: Staying healthy).

Sharing the nursery

If your cat jumps onto an object to investigate it for the first time when you bring it home (for example, the change table or cot or crib), allow them to investigate it thoroughly this first time. If you deny your cat the ability to investigate an object and possibly mark it with their pheromones, this can make them more anxious of the new object. Over time your cat will lose interest in the item and jump down off it. If they persist in jumping up onto something that you do not want them jumping on in the future (for example, the change table), despite it having been in the house for longer than a week, then start using your 'down' command training (see Chapter 8: Supervising, separating and training), followed by food rewards to encourage them to stay off the item. If you find your cat resting or sleeping in a location that is likely to be unsuitable when the baby arrives then you need to deny them access to that area when unsupervised (for example, shut the nursery door – see Chapter 8: Supervising, separating and training). If your cat will not be allowed unsupervised access to particular things once the baby is born, they should be off limits once the cat has done their initial investigation. Do not leave baby items lying around and easily accessible, in case your cat becomes destructive or chews on them.

Having a cat-scratching tree, shelf or perch in the nursery can be a great way for your cat to continue to interact with you while you are tending to your baby. This may be a low perch near the nursing chair or a higher perch next to the change table or cot or crib. This can help to deter your cat from jumping on the change table or into the crib, as they have an elevated position where they can watch what is going on without getting into areas that are out of bounds. Ideally, the perch should be at a height that allows you to pet or rub your cat while tending to your baby. A cat bed and tasty food rewards can also be regularly offered on these places to encourage your cat to relax there. This helps your cat know what they should and should not be doing in that room once the baby is present.

Place a cat bell on your cat's collar and purchase a baby monitor, even if your baby is always going to be near you; ensuring there are no inadvertent visitors in your baby's room can give extra security.

While you are in the birthing suite

Home alone

Organise early on for somebody to 'cat sit' your cat in your own home or to check in on the cat regularly while you are in the hospital or birthing centre. It should preferably be someone your cat knows well, to prevent additional stress. Boarding your cat or moving them to another house is a less suitable option, as there may be associated anxiety, particularly when they arrive back home to a totally changed environment. However, if this is necessary, have a trial run to ensure you and your cat feel comfortable with the arrangement. This allows your cat to become acquainted with the people and environment where they will be staying, which can make their stay less stressful.

Curious cats

Expectant parents may feel that they would like their 'first baby' to be present when their human baby arrives. This is not recommended. Birthing is often a stressful experience for both the mother and the newborn. Cats intuitively pick up on this stress and it is counterproductive for the first introduction to be in such an emotional setting.

12
Your baby is born!

Congratulations! You are now proud parents! Currently, Mum is still in hospital with the baby. Her partner now has some important tasks to perform to further prepare the cat at home.

The newborn smell

Smell is one of the cat's most important senses. Cats have an incredible sense of smell – far better than humans'! For this reason, your partner needs to bring home some of the following items to start introducing your baby to the cat: a soiled nappy or diaper, something that your baby has worn (for example, a jumpsuit, singlet, muslin wrap or blanket), a used breast pad and a used pacifier or bottle teat (if your baby uses these). These all contain important scents, enabling your cat to become acquainted with your baby even before they arrive home.

> **Smell is one of the cat's most important senses**

Before allowing your cat to sniff and investigate these objects, spray them with a small amount of Feliway spray at least 30 minutes before introducing them to your cat (see 'Feliway' in Chapter 9: Staying healthy). By spraying Feliway on the new baby items, they appear to the cat to be more familiar, which will help to lessen your cat's

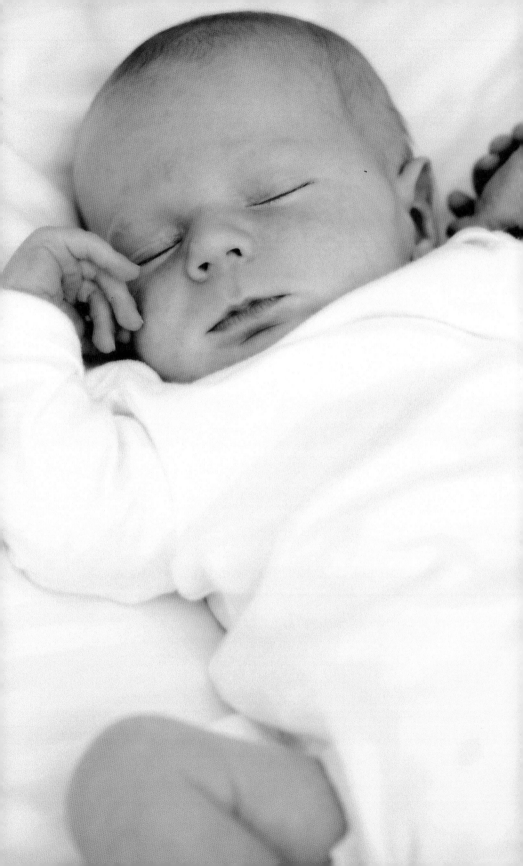

anxiety towards them. Be sure to wash the items after using Feliway, if they are to be used again for your baby.

Allow the cat to sniff and investigate these items and reward them lavishly with tasty treats, pets or a period of play with their favourite toy, for relaxed behaviour (behaviour group A). If they show some anxiety towards a particular item (behaviour group B) then try and distract them away with something they enjoy (for example, treats or a toy). Then reintroduce the item while they are focused on the treat or toy. Ideally they should now show signs from behaviour group A. If after several attempts they continue to show signs outlined in behaviour group B or they show signs outlined in behaviour groups C or D towards the item, then you need to seek assistance from an appropriate veterinarian. Do not leave these items lying around unsupervised.

Wrap a pretend baby in a blanket or clothing that your newborn baby has worn, and perform a couple of sessions with the baby soundtracks in specific locations, as outlined earlier in steps 4 and 5. At the same time, talk to your cat in an upbeat voice, telling them about the new arrival and using your baby's name.

Plan ahead and choose a particular blanket or muslin wrap to place your baby in to bring them home. Before you do, and if your cat will allow it, wipe the outside of the blanket over the cat, focusing particularly on stroking their whiskers, cheeks and body. This is where familiarising pheromones are produced by cats. If possible, this wrap or blanket should be the outer wrap or garment your baby has on when they first arrive. In this way the baby will already smell familiar to the cat and this will help to ease anxiety. If your cat does not like being wiped with the baby's blanket then spray the outside of the blanket or wrap with Feliway spray. Allow the spray to dry before wrapping your baby.

Meeting the baby

You now have your cat prepared in the best way possible for the impending arrival. They know what sounds to expect (via the baby sounds and toy noises), they know what the little person smells like and they have adapted to the new household routine. Now it is time to meet the family!

The day your baby is due to arrive home, you might try delaying your cat's normal feed, or halving the amount, as this may make them more accepting of treats or food when you arrive home with your baby. *Do not do this if your cat is likely to become frustrated, difficult to manage, highly demanding or possibly even aggressive when they have not been fed.* Feeding tasty food at this time means your cat will associate good things with the baby's arrival right from the start.

Have somebody that your cat likes and knows well come and play with them for a period before you arrive home, to tire them slightly. *Do not do this if your cat remains highly aroused after playing.* When Mum first arrives home from hospital, your cat will be very excited to see her again. They will also be excited to see her partner, who may have been away too. An overly excited cat greeting you and your new baby for the first time could cause problems. Have someone, other than you or your partner, cuddle your baby outside the house while you both go in and greet your cat. In this way, you can give your cat your full attention without worrying about the cat hurting your baby. Once they are calm, introductions can begin. Limit the number of people present at the first meeting.

> Good things should happen to your cat when your baby is around

The most important thing to remember when your cat meets your baby is that good things should always happen to your cat whenever your baby is around. Whenever your baby is present, give your cat tasty food rewards, loads of petting or a period of play.

Cats are unlikely to scratch or injure a baby in this first meeting. It's more likely your cat will be frightened by a sudden noise or movement from your baby. Try to minimise this by having your baby tightly wrapped or well swaddled to avoid sudden arm or leg movements startling your cat.

If you are particularly concerned about how your cat may behave, or worried that you will be unable to control your cat, place them in their carrier or put their harness and leash on before you bring the baby into the house. Training to do this should be completed well in advance so it does not distress your cat (See Chapter 8: Supervising, separating and training). If you do not want to put your cat in their carrier, prepare a large thick towel by spraying it with Feliway. You can use this towel to corral your cat or pick them up if they continually show highly undesirable behaviour towards the baby (that is, behaviour groups B, C or D), and remove them to a separate area without injuries.

Choose a quiet room with few distractions for the first introductions. One partner should squat or kneel down on the floor with their back resting against a wall. The area in front of this person should be free of couches, tables or other elevated areas. They should hold the baby in their arms. This enables easy control of the amount of access your cat initially has to your baby. Often when someone sits down on a chair or couch, the cat sees this as an invitation to jump onto their lap. This is not ideal. Also if you sit too close to a table or elevated object the cat is likely to get up onto it to have better access to the baby, and this can be problematic. The other partner should monitor your cat and be prepared to distract them with food rewards or a toy or even carry them away (using the towel) if their behaviour becomes an issue (behaviour groups B, C or D).

Both parents need to take a deep breath and try to relax for this introduction. If you are anxious or distressed, your cat will sense this. Talk gently to your cat while petting and stroking them. Under

strict supervision, encourage them to smell and investigate your baby. Reward them for appropriate behaviour with food rewards, pets and an upbeat, calm voice. Do not force your cat to interact if they do not appear to want to, and do not hold or dangle the child in front of your cat.

> ## Gently encourage your cat to investigate the baby

Responses to a new baby vary greatly. Some cats will appear interested for a few seconds and then quickly lose interest. If your cat prefers to run away from the baby, allow them to escape and investigate the baby in their own time. Some cats will just ignore the new arrival. Initial curiosity can be intense but usually decreases over a few days. If your cat is overly inquisitive, distract them away with a toy or highly valued food item. Some cats may become anxious in the presence of the baby and it may take some time for your cat to become used to having a baby around, so be patient. If you are concerned about how your cat is reacting, seek assistance from an appropriate veterinarian.

Remember to take it very slowly. Do not rush the meeting – they have a lifetime to be friends. Be pleased and reward your cat if they are calm, relaxed or slightly inquisitive (behaviour group A) in your baby's presence – this is desirable. Offer lots of praise, treats or play whenever your cat comes near the baby.

> ## Take it slowly – they have a lifetime to be friends

Never punish your cat around your baby. Your main aim is to foster a good relationship. Make highly enjoyable and fun things happen for your cat whenever your baby is present. If the cat is showing signs of anxiety, fear or aggression (behaviour groups B, C or D), simply remove them to a safe, secure area and try again later when things are calmer.

Olive, the super-relaxed cat

I visited Andrew and Jo for an urgent house call for their five-year-old cat, Olive. She was hissing whenever Andrew approached her, and would also run away and hide whenever their new baby, Claudia, cried. I was surprised, as Olive was one of the most relaxed cats I had seen at the veterinary clinic.

Andrew and Jo admitted that Olive had probably never seen or heard a baby before and, due to a lack of time, they had done nothing to prepare Olive for Claudia's arrival. Guiltily, they admitted that they had thought Olive, being such a relaxed cat, would cope just fine. I must admit, I'd thought so, too.

They told me that, a week ago, when they had first brought Claudia home, they immediately introduced her to Olive. Olive was very apprehensive about Claudia and reluctant to approach her, so Andrew had picked Olive up and brought her closer to Claudia to encourage an interaction. At this point, Claudia started to cry, and at one stage she had even flailed her arms around. Olive then started hissing and struggling to get out of Andrew's grasp. Andrew eventually let go of Olive and shooed her away. Now Andrew could not approach Olive without her running away or hissing. This clearly was not the relaxed introduction they were hoping for.

Our first priority was to allow Olive time to settle. Cats often stay agitated for long periods and continual approaches by Andrew were likely to be upsetting her further. Currently, Olive was spending a lot of time in the spare bedroom, away from the family and new noises. This was to be an Olive-only area for the next few weeks. We moved her bedding, food, water and a litter box into this room so she would feel more comfortable. A pheromone diffuser was placed in her room to help settle her. For the next ten days, Andrew and Jo were only to go into Olive's room to change the litter box and provide food and water. They were not to approach Olive unless she chose to initiate the contact.

After ten days, Andrew and Jo said that Olive was much calmer and was now approaching them around the house when Claudia was asleep. As soon as Claudia would wake up or cry, Olive would scurry back to her room. Andrew said that Olive was no longer hissing at him or running away, and their relationship had been restored. Their concern now was how to make Olive happier with Claudia's presence.

We discussed how this could take some time, and that Olive would benefit from some anxiety-lowering medication to help her to relax around Claudia. Andrew and Jo agreed. We also started to associate good things happening for Olive when Claudia was awake. When Claudia woke up from her naps, they would toss a Kong® filled with tuna paste into Olive's room on the way to Claudia's room. Olive loved tuna paste, and placing it in a Kong toy would make it a longer-lasting tasty treat. Olive also loved chasing feathers on a stick, and Andrew or Jo were to have periods of dedicated playtime, when Claudia was awake, encouraging Olive out from her room and into the living area by chasing the feather. We also discussed environmental enrichment as another way to decrease Olive's anxiety.

Three months later I revisited Andrew and Jo to get an update. Olive was now out in the living area chilling on the couch, while Claudia was playing on a mat on the floor. Olive still didn't like it when Claudia was screaming her loudest (she had a real set of lungs!) and she would again retreat to her room. But Olive was definitely spending more and more time with the whole family, and her owners were pleased with her progress.

I have to say that super-relaxed Olive was the first cat that truly highlighted for me the importance of a calm and slow first introduction. Olive and Claudia have a lifetime to become friends, and a much more controlled, less stressful introduction would have gone a long way to starting them off on good terms.

Meeting problems

If your cat becomes frightened or hisses at your baby, distract them with food or play or physically separate them, or remove your baby to another room, until they settle. Remember that cats can stay fearful or agitated for long periods (even days!), so ensure they are relaxed and calm before trying again. If your cat shows signs outlined in behaviour groups B, C or D, they may be unsure about your baby. Try again at a later time, this time with a larger distance between your cat and your baby. You may want to separate the two by placing your cat in their carrier while rewarding relaxed behaviour. It may help to allow visual contact only, with separation, while you work on good things happening when the baby is visible. It's important to keep trying, rather than isolating your cat from your baby. Try to stay calm and relaxed.

If, after repeated attempted introductions, even from a distance, your cat will not calm down or consistently shows signs outlined in behaviour group B or C, you need to seek assistance from an appropriate veterinarian.

In rare cases, a cat will crouch low, stalk and stare (behaviour group D) at your baby during the introduction and be unable to break away from their fixation on the baby. They may become highly focused on the baby, even to just the sound of the baby, but they are often further stimulated by movement. It is very hard to distract a cat from this focus, and the fixation may occur every time they are in the vicinity of the infant. Cats displaying these behaviours need to be safely and securely separated from the baby immediately, and advice sought from an appropriate veterinarian.

Creating harmony

Your main responsibility is never to leave your baby unsupervised with your cat. Initially, when both parents are home and your cat and baby are together or in the same room, one of you should attend to your baby and the other to your cat. Vary this between the two of you, and try to ensure both of you give your cat equal attention. Try to include your cat in day-to-day activities as much as possible so they do not feel neglected. Do not give your cat attention only when your baby is out of the room and then ignore them when your baby is present. This may cause your cat to associate a lack of attention with the presence of your baby, which is not desirable. Whenever your baby is present, praise and stroke your cat and give them tasty food rewards, toys they like to play with or a chewy treat. Whenever your baby cries, try to remain calm and unrushed to avoid startling your cat.

> ## Never leave your baby unsupervised with your cat

When only one of you is home in the first few weeks, if you do not feel you have good control over your cat, they should be confined in a safe and secure area with a tasty food-release toy or similar. It is difficult for one person to monitor everyone in the house at the same time, so, ideally, your cat should be in an area where they can see you and your baby, unless they are showing signs outlined in behaviour groups B, C or D. Enabling your cat to see the baby and you but still be separated means that you can monitor your cat's response to the baby and also reward them with treats and praise when they are behaving appropriately. Your cat is also likely to remain calmer and feel like a part of the family if they can still see you.

Eventually, your cat may sociably follow you around the house and engage with you while you attend to your baby. This is fine and bodes well for future interactions between your child and your cat. If you need to leave the room, safely and securely separate your baby and cat, even if one or both of them are sleeping.

Visiting with your baby

When you visit relatives or friends who own a cat or dog, remain vigilant at all times. Their pets may not have had the same exposure to babies and may react differently from your pet. It might be helpful to suggest they also read *Tell Your Cat You're Pregnant* and/or *Tell Your Dog You're Pregnant* to ensure that their pets are also ready for the new visitor.

Guests

You are likely to have lots of visitors when your new baby arrives, including family, friends and health-care providers. Some sociable cats may enjoy the extra attention they receive from visitors, whereas others may become overwhelmed, especially if they are not used to it. Cats should always have access to their cat-only safe haven whenever they need to retreat from visitors (see Chapter 8: Supervising, separating and training).

Ideally, unfamiliar guests should be encouraged to ignore your cat unless your cat actively solicits attention from them. If your cat does solicit attention and you are unsure how your cat will behave, instruct your guests to only pet them around the head, as some cats may not enjoy having other areas handled by strangers. If your cat seems slightly timid (behaviour group B) then try to encourage them to interact by getting the guests to throw some tasty treats near your cat. You may need assistance from an appropriate veterinarian if your cat is aggressive or extremely fearful (behaviour group C).

Alert guests to the presence of your cat by placing a sign on the front door (for example, 'Please don't let the cat out'). Keep in mind that excited guests may become distracted and not notice your sign!

Two or more cats

Managing two or more cats is more complex than managing one, and you will know that each has a different personality. It is preferable to perform all the assessments and training outlined in this book with each cat separately to ascertain their individual reaction before reassessing all the cats together. This includes steps 1 to 5 described earlier (with the sounds) and the initial introductions when your baby first arrives home.

Getting another cat

Getting another cat to keep the first cat company may seem like a good idea when a baby comes along as you may have less time to devote to your cat. Some cats do enjoy the company of another cat, but others prefer to be solitary and will be actively aggressive to a newcomer in the house. In this case the introduction of a new cat or kitten will cause more issues than it will solve. Even cats who have lived with another cat their whole life may not automatically get along with a new cat or kitten introduced into the house.

Littermates that have been raised together are more likely to get along than unfamiliar cats. Do not introduce a new cat or kitten to the house to keep your cat company while you are pregnant – you may be putting yourself at increased risk of toxoplasmosis (see Chapter 3: Toxoplasmosis). There are other more suitable ways of keeping your cat company or occupied when you are expecting a baby (see Chapter 10: Preparing your cat).

Appropriate interactions with toddlers

Some cats become more concerned about children when they are mobile than when they are tiny babies. A crawling or toddling child can take a cat by surprise, and his or her squeals and shrieks can be frightening for a cat. Providing places for your cat to escape to is even more important at this stage (for example, a cat-only safe haven or an

elevated resting place). This will allow your cat to avoid being continually followed, cornered and perhaps feeling pestered by your child.

> **A crawling baby can easily surprise or scare a cat**

Your baby or child is likely to be very interested in your cat. In fact, many children's first few words are related to pets or animals. Just as you don't allow your cat to have free access to your child, your child must be supervised and taught to behave properly around pets. Grabbing, chasing, pulling or other investigatory behaviours on your child's part, while completely normal, are not appropriate.

Begin by teaching your child how to properly approach and touch your cat: calmly, quietly and gently. Your cat should not be expected to tolerate shouting or grabbing; so, if your child becomes overly excited, remove your child from the situation and try again another time. Both your cat and your child should learn that interactions can be fun and rewarding, not scary and painful!

Your cat (and baby) sitter

It may be several weeks now since you brought your baby home and you may be thinking about occasionally leaving your baby in the care of a relative, friend or babysitter. It is important not to forget the 'number two' baby now – your cat! Ideally the carer should be a person well known to the cat so as not to stress them by their presence.

Create a list of checkpoints that pertain to the daily management of your cat. It can be helpful to do this now, even if a babysit is not planned, as it is likely you will be more concerned about your baby's needs and forget to discuss your cat's needs on the actual day. Advanced planning can avoid this. Things to consider mentioning to the sitter are:

- Never leave the cat and baby together unsupervised.
- Use the food rewards provided to reward correct behaviours.
- Do not use physical or verbal punishment on the cat.
- Use the same words that you use to instruct the cat (for example, 'go to your bed' and 'down').
- How the cat and baby should be safely and securely separated if the carer needs to leave the room.
- Do not allow the cat in the baby's room when the baby is sleeping.
- Leave the cat alone when they are in their cat-only safe haven.
- How to correctly clean the litter box (if needed).
- Whether and at what times your cat is allowed outside.

Things to remember

- Read the entire book before you start preparing your cat.
- Never leave your baby and cat together unsupervised.
- Start preparing your cat as early as possible.
- Educate yourself about toxoplasmosis and how it relates to your cat.
- Address any aggression or toileting issues early.
- Teach your cat 'down' and 'go to your bed'.
- Stop all physical and verbal punishment or reprimands.
- Assess how your cat currently reacts around babies.
- Create a cat-only safe haven.
- Create a safe and secure area where you can separate your cat from your baby.
- Decide early where your baby will sleep and how to keep your cat out of this area.
- Monitor your cat's body language using behaviour groups A, B, C and D.
- Work slowly through steps 1 to 5 with your cat using the baby sounds and toy noises.
- Set up realistic feeding, petting, grooming and play schedules.
- Increase the amount of suitable environmental enrichment for your cat.
- Introduce your cat early to all the new baby-related items in the house and nursery.
- After the baby is born, bring home some worn baby clothes from the hospital for your cat to smell.
- Take the first introduction very slowly. Do not force your cat on your baby or vice versa.
- Make fun things happen to your cat whenever the baby is present.
- Look forward to the benefits of your extended family.

Further help

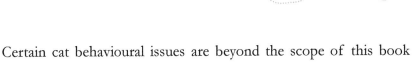

Certain cat behavioural issues are beyond the scope of this book and some problems are more serious and require assistance from an appropriate veterinarian. An 'appropriate veterinarian', when mentioned in this book, is a veterinarian with a professional interest in animal behaviour.

Appropriate veterinarians (veterinarians with a professional interest in animal behaviour)[*]

These are veterinarians who have undertaken further (postgraduate) study or passed examinations in animal behaviour or both. They have a more extensive knowledge of behavioural problems in cats and how to treat them than other veterinarians. They may or may not be veterinary behaviourists.

- ❖ The Veterinary Behaviour Chapter of the Australian and New Zealand College of Veterinary Scientists (ANZCVS) **www.anzcvs.org.au**
- ❖ Delta Professional Dog Trainers Association (DPDTA) – has a listing of Australian appropriate veterinarians who can assist with cat behaviour problems. **www.dpdta.com.au/vet-behaviourist**
- ❖ American College of Veterinary Behaviorists (ACVB) **www.dacvb.com**

[*] Websites listed in this book are for reference only, and neither the author nor publisher endorses their contents. Websites are correct at time of printing.

❖ American Veterinary Society of Animal Behavior (AVSAB) **www.avsabonline.org**

❖ Association of Pet Behaviour Counsellors (APBC) **www.apbc.org.uk**

❖ European College of Animal Welfare and Behavioural Medicine (ECAWBM) **www.ecawbm.com**

Tell us about your experience

I hope that this book has helped you cope easily and smoothly with the addition of another very special member of your family. If you would like to send a photo of your new larger family and details of your experience, please go to our Facebook page '**Baby and Pet**' or send an email to info@babyandpet.com.au. No photos of unsupervised cats and babies, please!

For updates on this book and the latest research on cats and babies please 'like' our Facebook page '**Baby and Pet**'. You can also follow the author, Dr Kirkham on Twitter (**@VetBehaviourist**).

For those pregnant owners who are lucky enough to also own a dog, be sure to read *Tell Your Dog You're Pregnant: An essential guide for dog owners who are expecting a baby*, to assist in preparing your dog for the impending arrival. Please go to **www.babyandpet.com.au** for further information.

About the author

Dr Lewis Kirkham, a veterinarian with further qualifications in animal behaviour, has a lifelong fascination with pets and their interaction with their owners. Since graduating as a veterinarian from the University of Melbourne in Victoria, Australia, Dr Kirkham has worked in a variety of practices in both Australia and the United Kingdom.

In 2004, he founded Animal Behaviour Solutions, a company that provides private counselling and behavioural advice for pet owners. Through this company, Dr Kirkham has assisted numerous pets and their owners in the assessment and management of behaviour problems. He is also a consultant to local and international zoos and sanctuaries on exotic species' behavioural problems.

Dr Kirkham regularly features on TV, radio and online media regarding behavioural problems in pets. He contributes to the *Age, Herald Sun*, the *Daily Telegraph*, the *Courier Mail*, the *Advertiser* and the *Australian* newspapers, *Dogs Life, Living and Lifestyle, Oriental BQ Weekly, Woolworths Baby and Toddler Club* and *Urban Animal* magazines. He has also published in the *Australian Veterinary Journal*. He is a member of the Australian and New Zealand College of Veterinary Scientists and the American Veterinary Society of Animal Behavior.

The birth of his two daughters ignited his passion for educating expectant parents about the smooth transition from a child-free cat or dog-owning family to a larger family with a new baby. Following the worldwide success of Dr Kirkham's first book, *Tell Your Dog You're Pregnant: An essential guide for dog owners who are expecting a baby*, he became aware of the widespread demand for a book to assist pregnant owners of cats, hence the arrival of *Tell Your Cat You're Pregnant: An essential guide for cat owners who are expecting a baby*.

Currently Dr Kirkham divides his time between his family, private veterinary practice, companion and exotic animal behaviour referrals and online veterinary support.

Don't forget your dog!

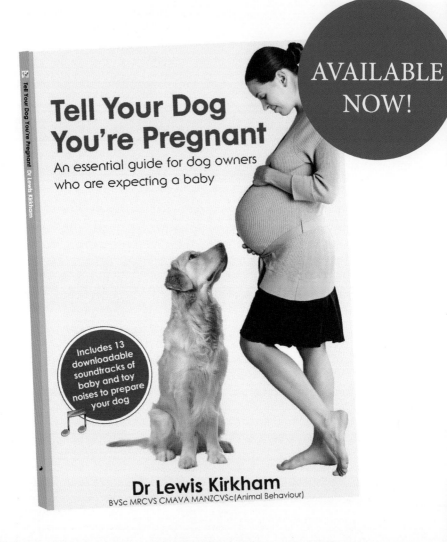

Printed in Great Britain
by Amazon